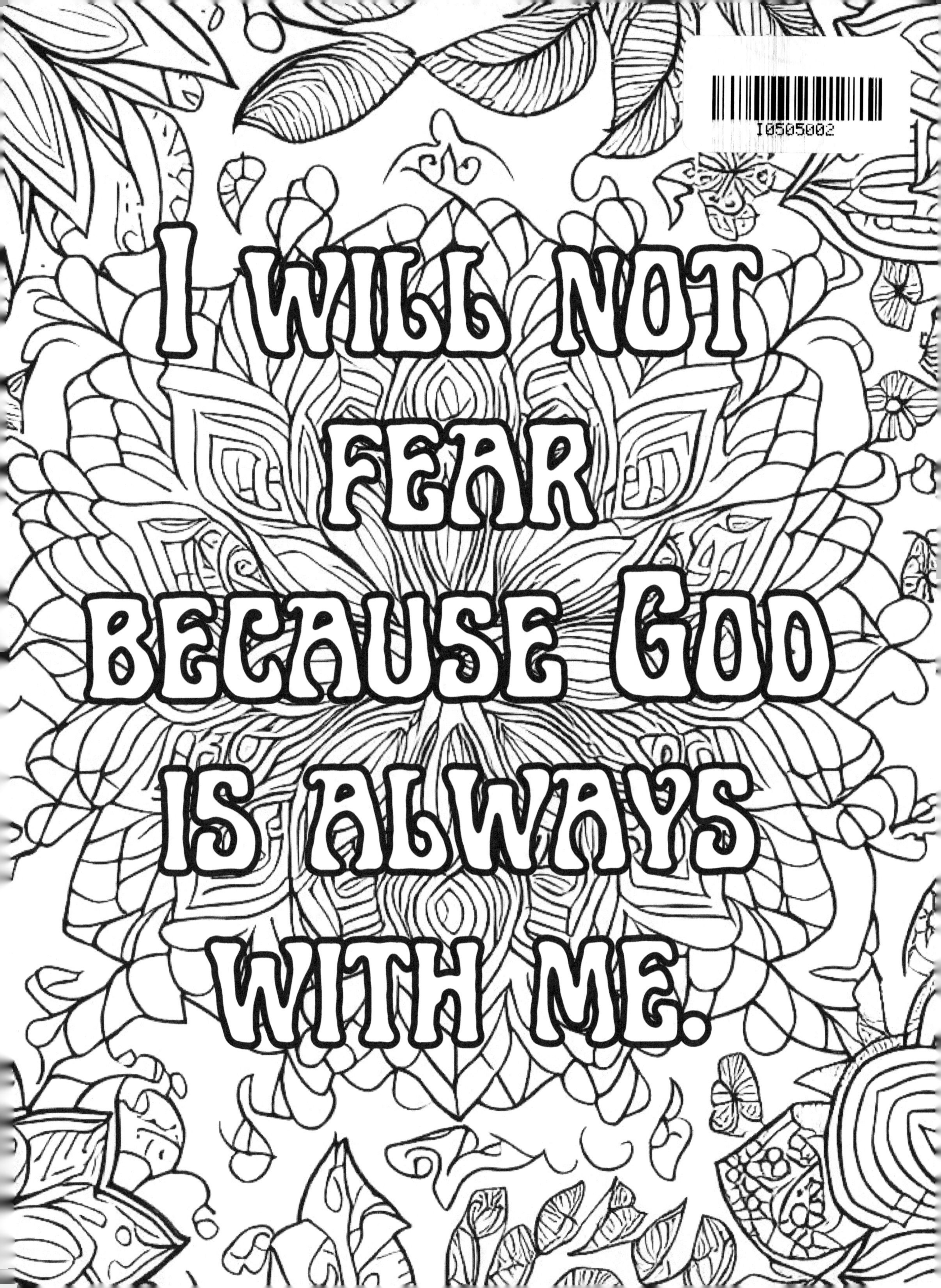
I WILL NOT
FEAR
BECAUSE GOD
IS ALWAYS
WITH ME.

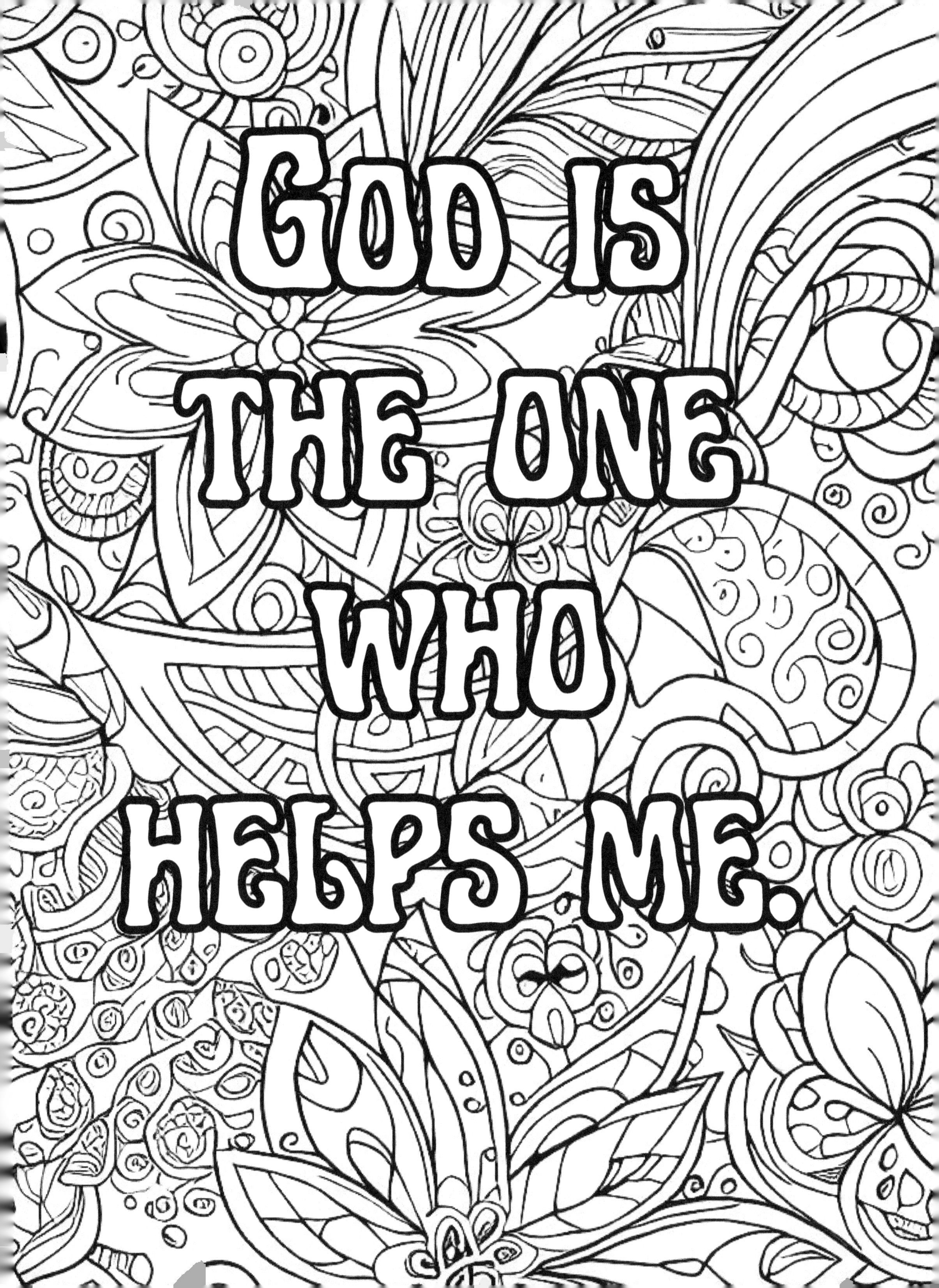
GOD IS
THE ONE
WHO
HELPS ME.

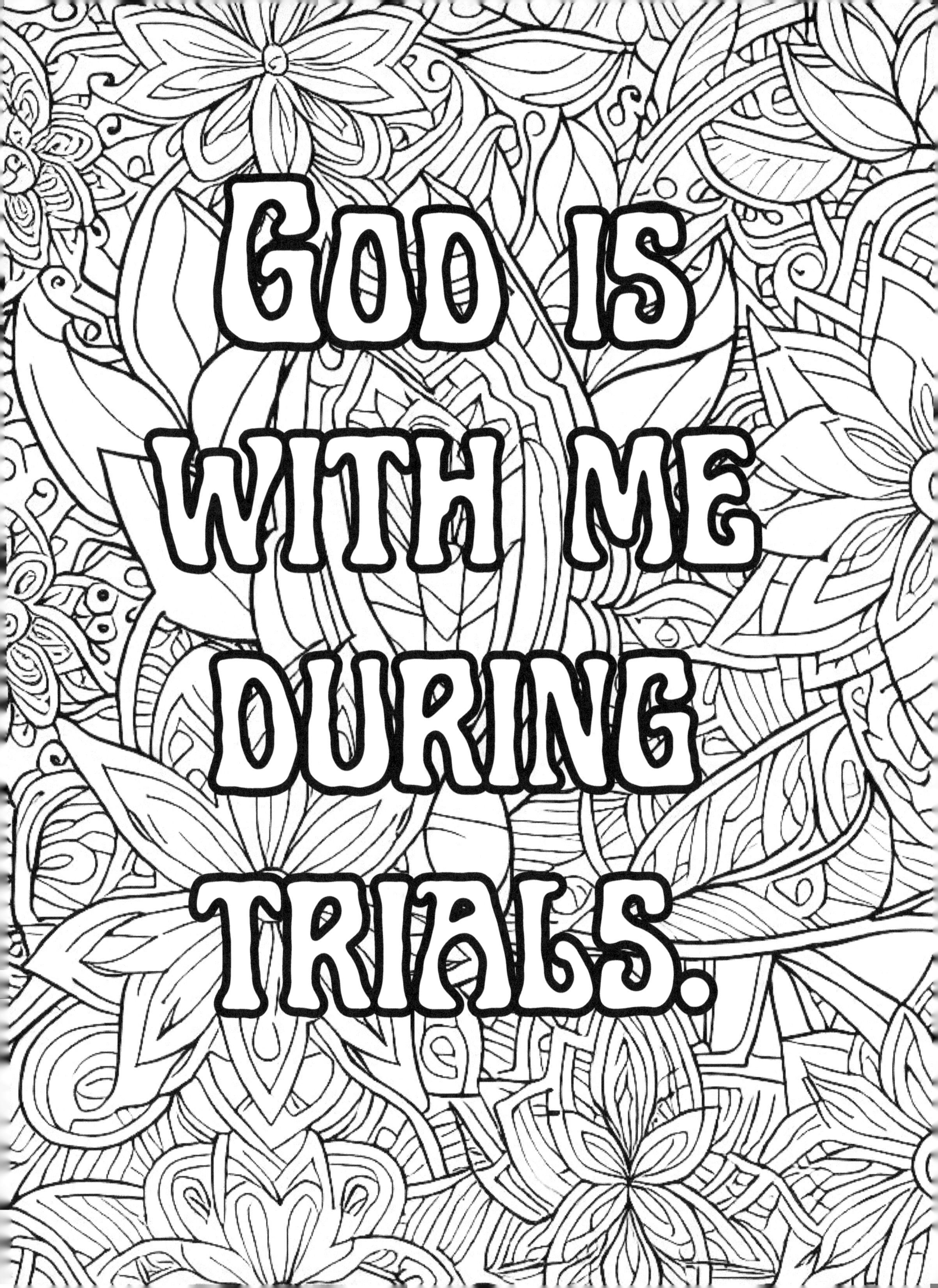
GOD IS
WITH ME
DURING
TRIALS.

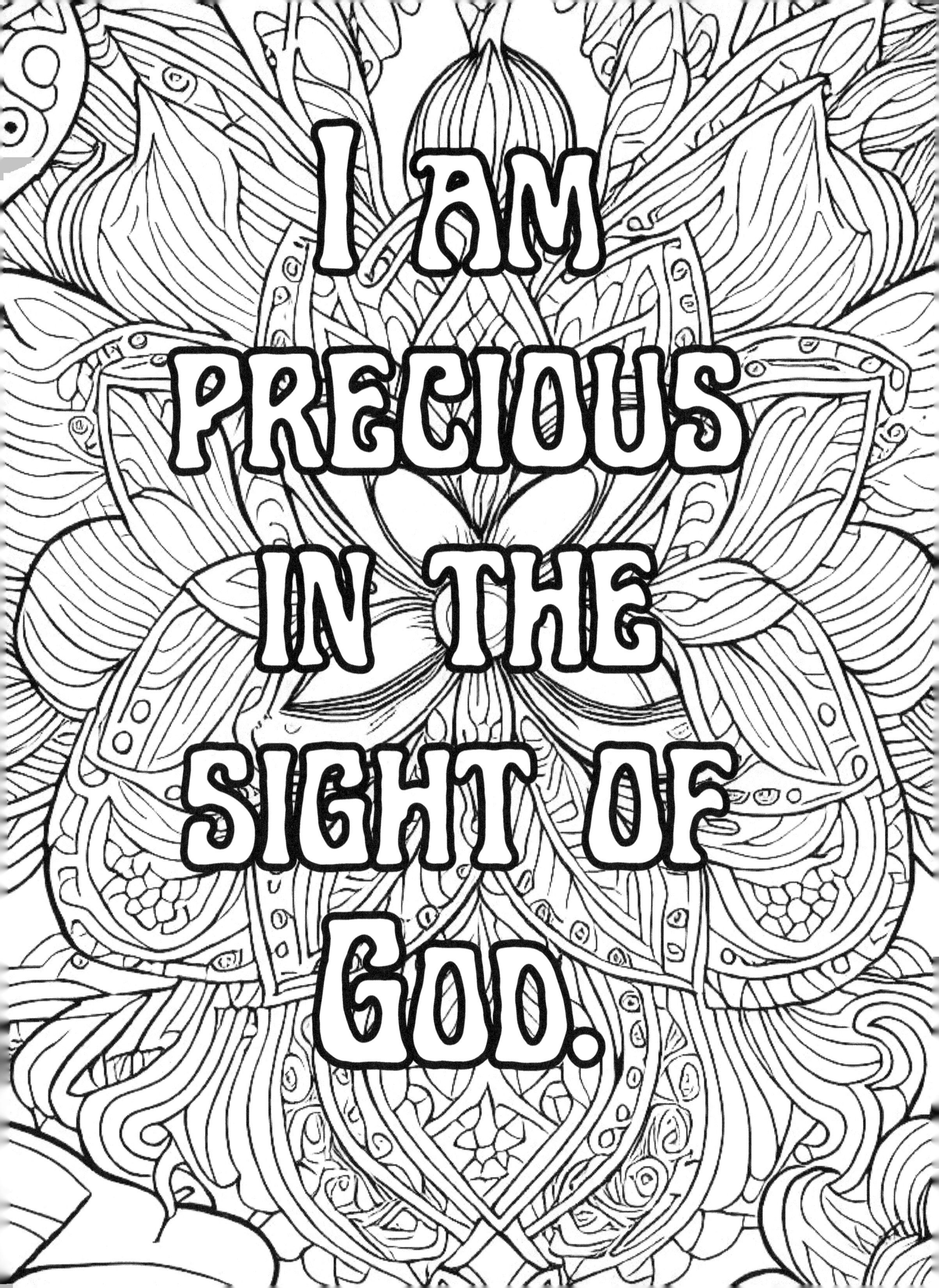
I AM
PRECIOUS
IN THE
SIGHT OF
GOD.

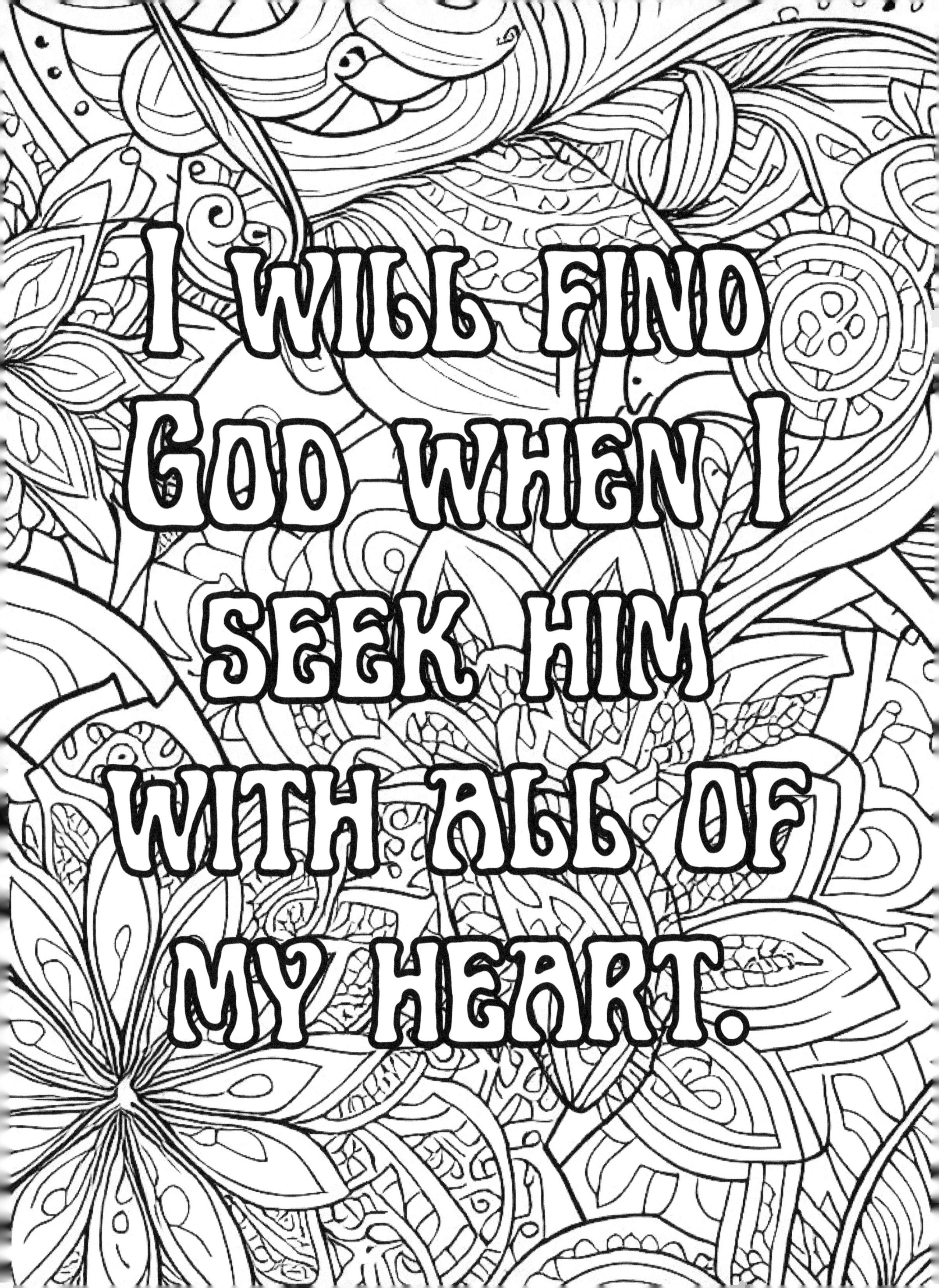
I WILL FIND GOD WHEN I SEEK HIM WITH ALL OF MY HEART.

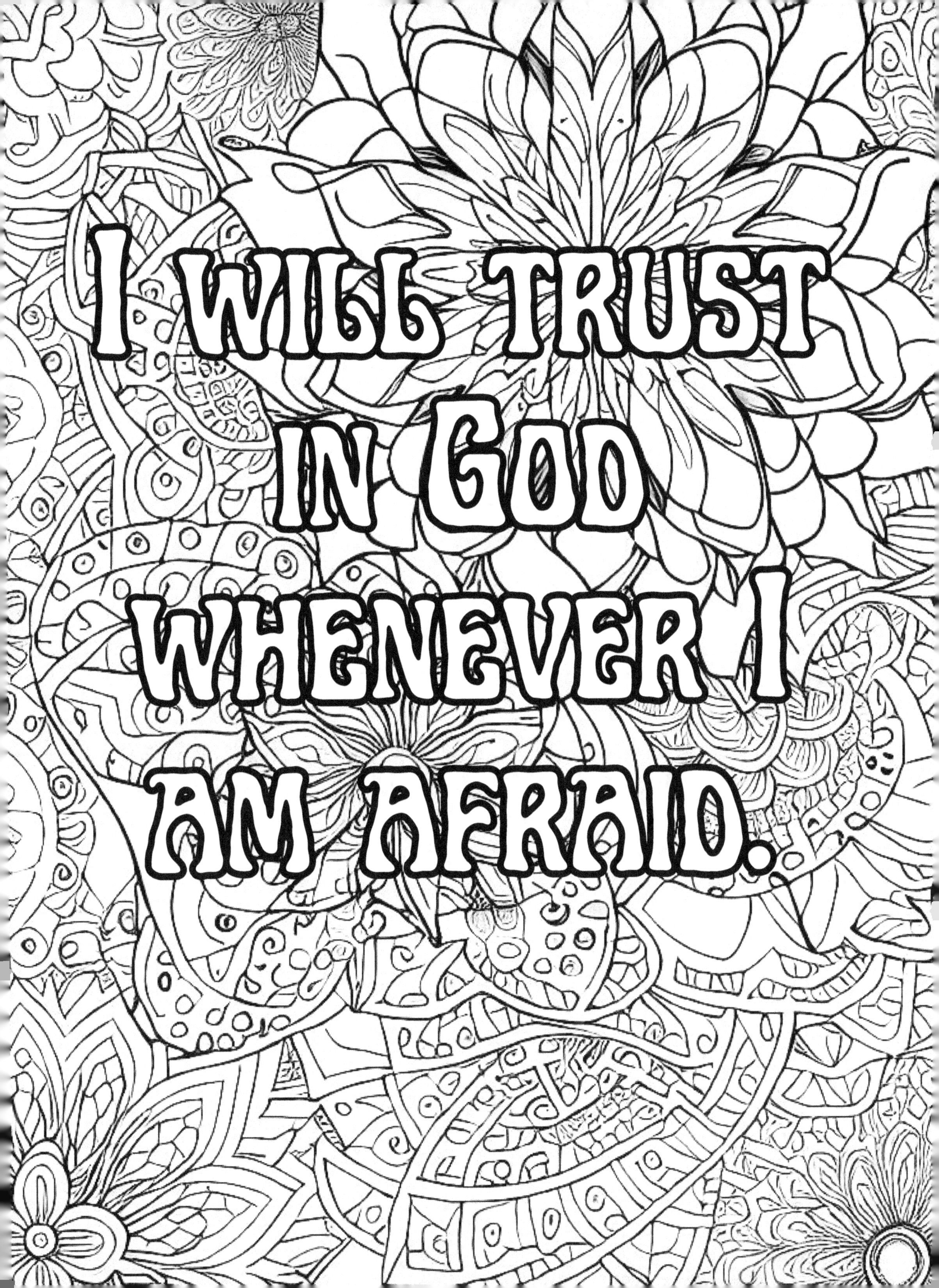
I will trust
in God
whenever I
am afraid.

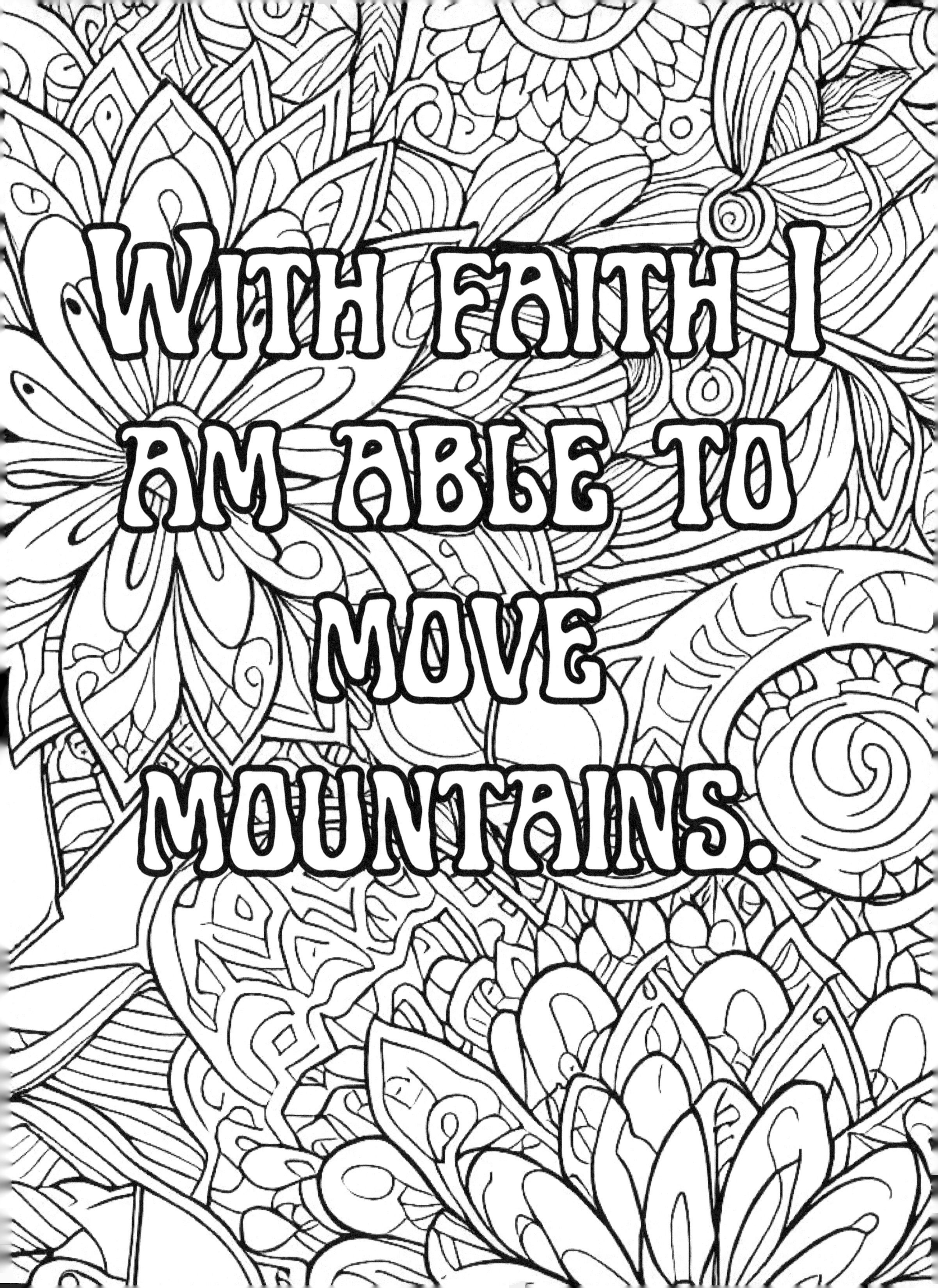
With faith I
am able to
move
mountains.

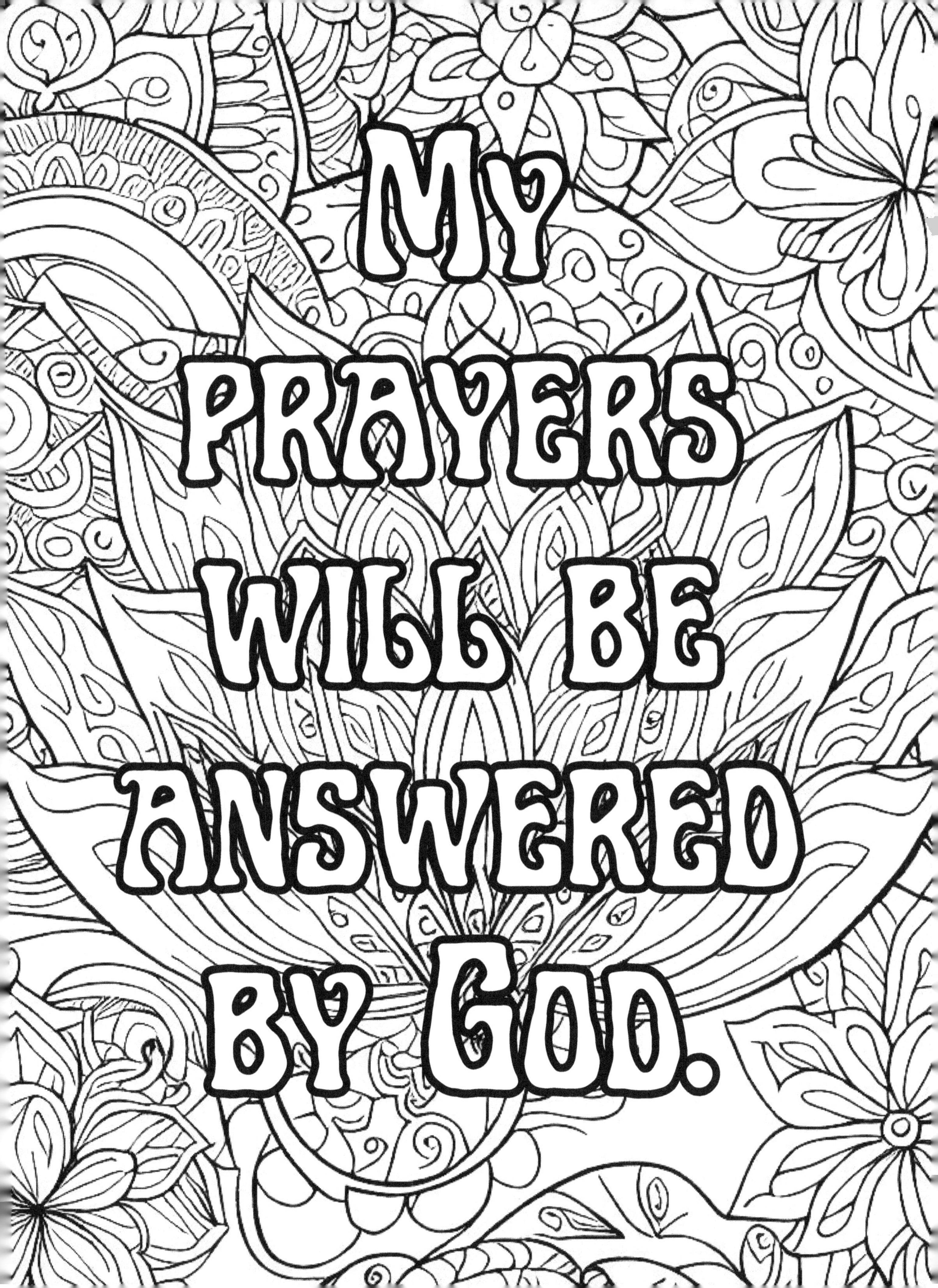
My PRAYERS WILL BE ANSWERED BY GOD.

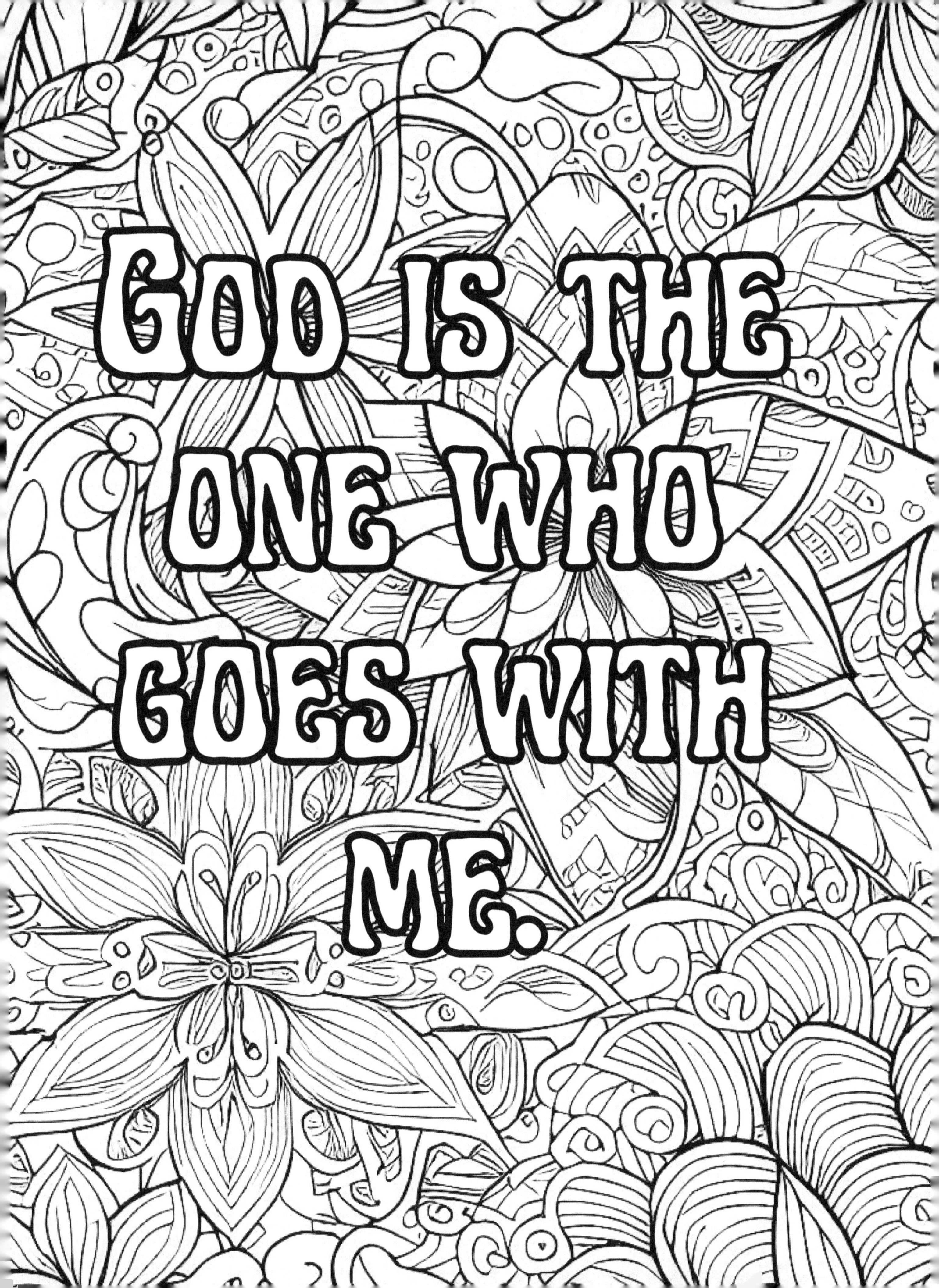
GOD IS THE ONE WHO GOES WITH ME.

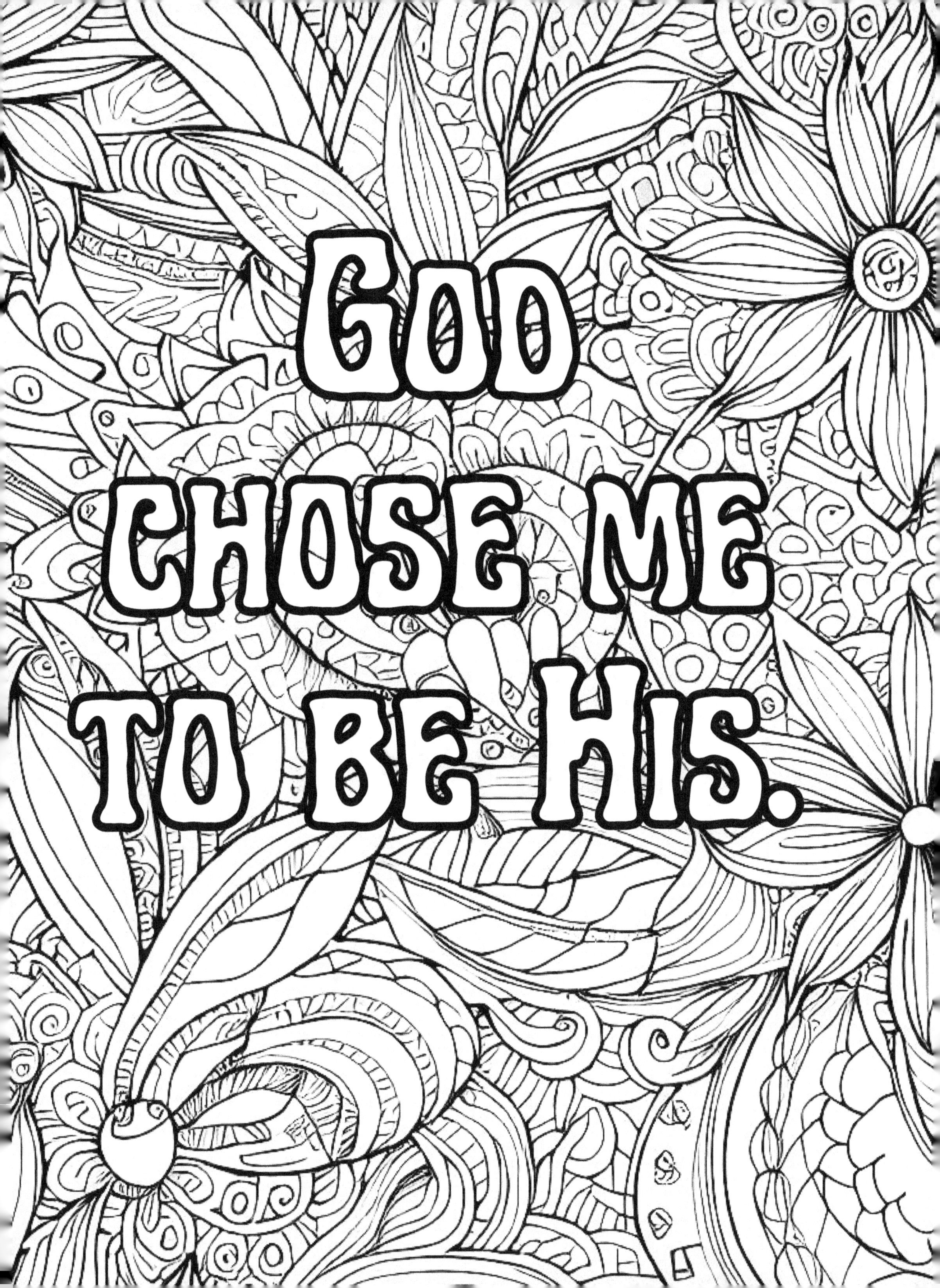
GOD
CHOSE ME
TO BE HIS.

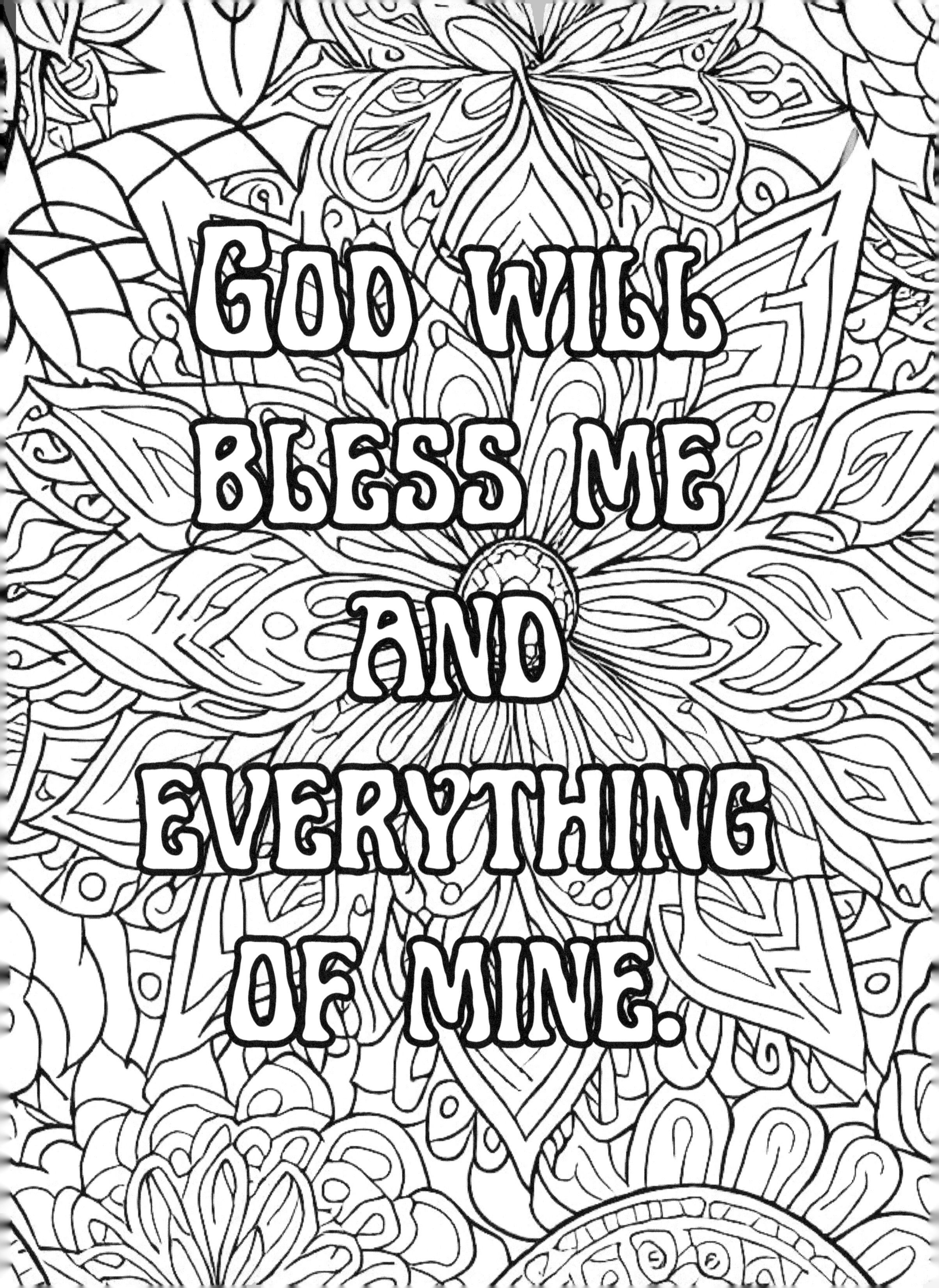
GOD WILL
BLESS ME
AND
EVERYTHING
OF MINE.

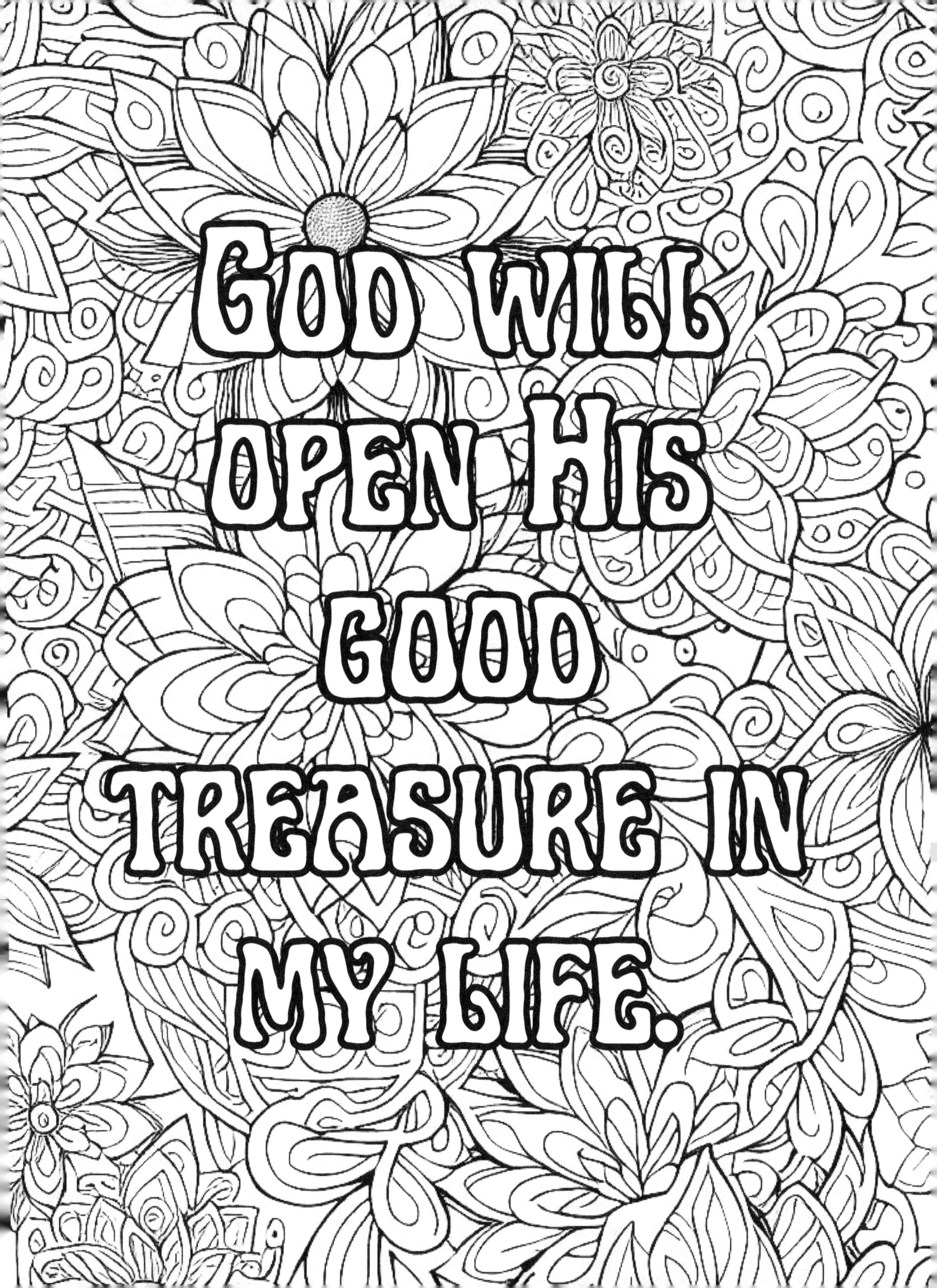
God will
open His
good
treasure in
my life.

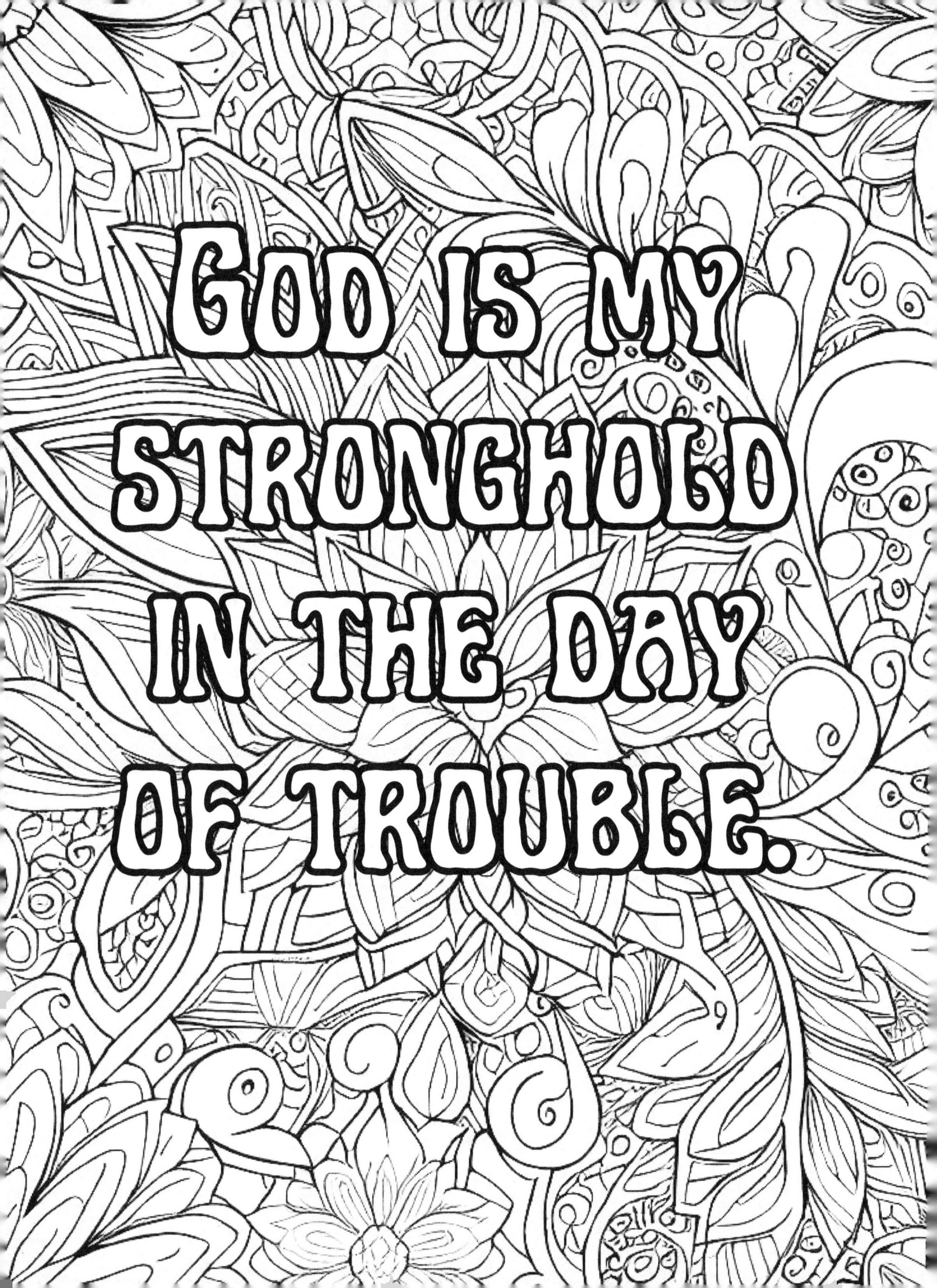
GOD IS MY
STRONGHOLD
IN THE DAY
OF TROUBLE.

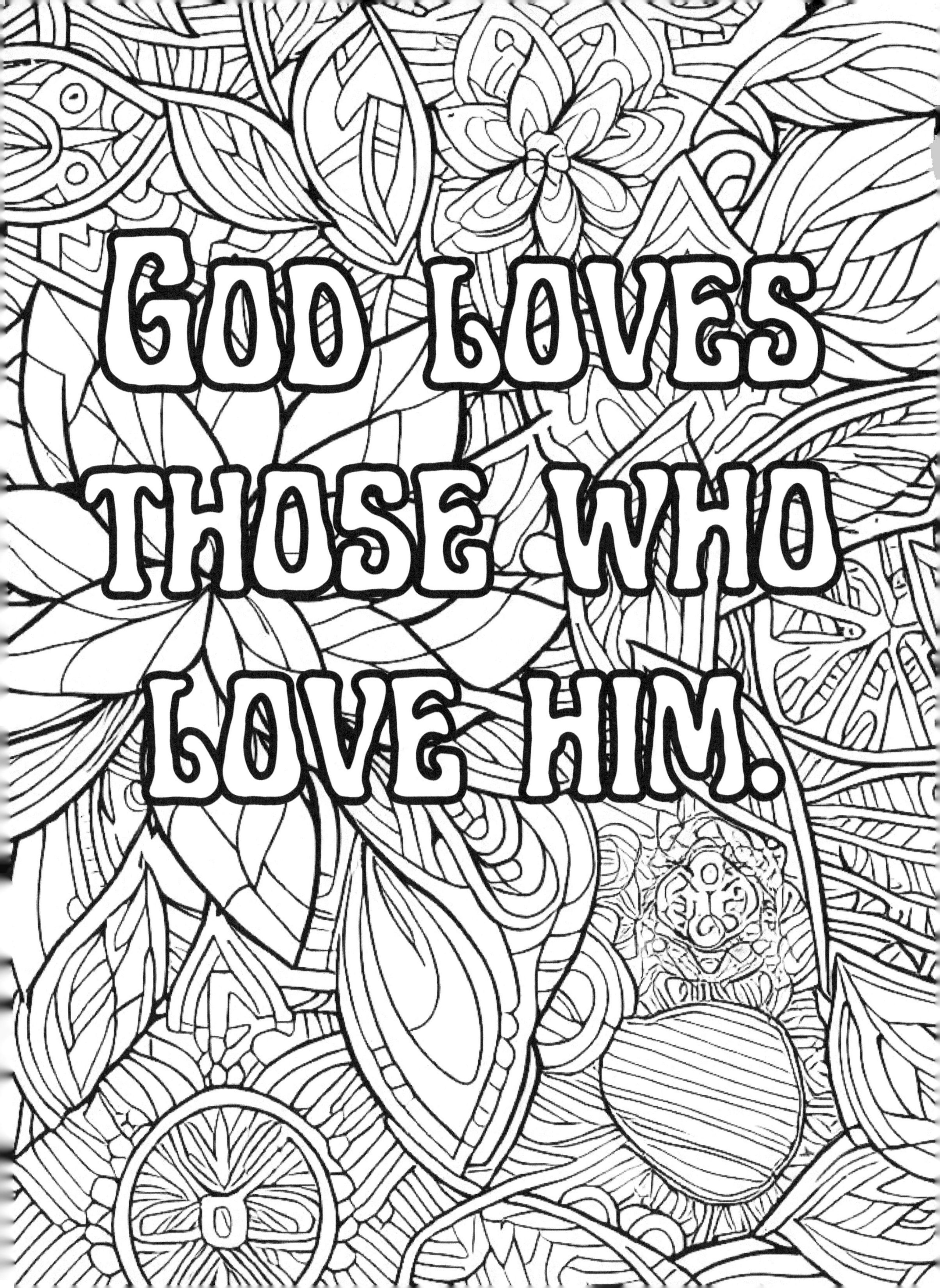
GOD LOVES
THOSE WHO
LOVE HIM.

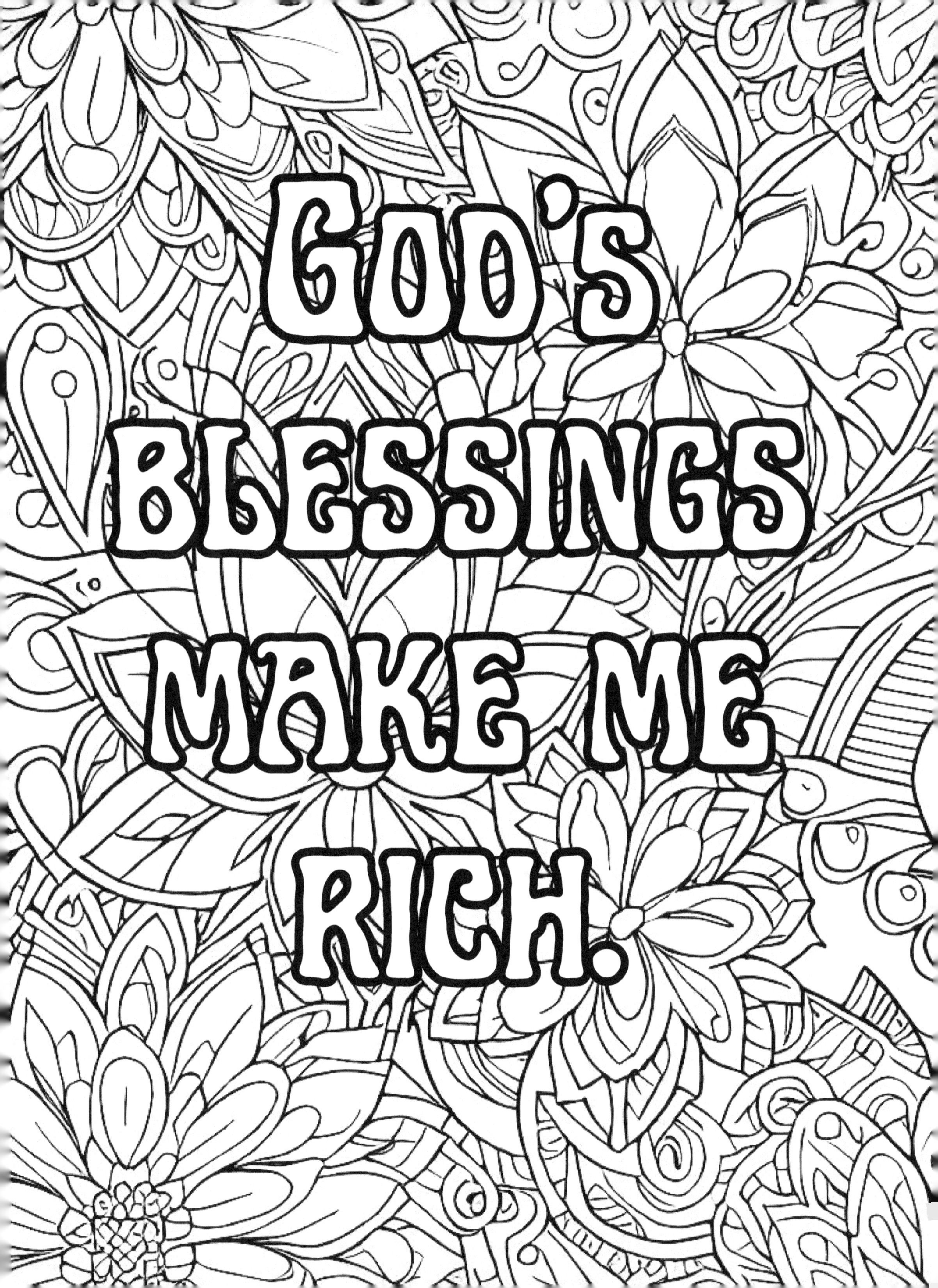
GOD'S BLESSINGS MAKE ME RICH.

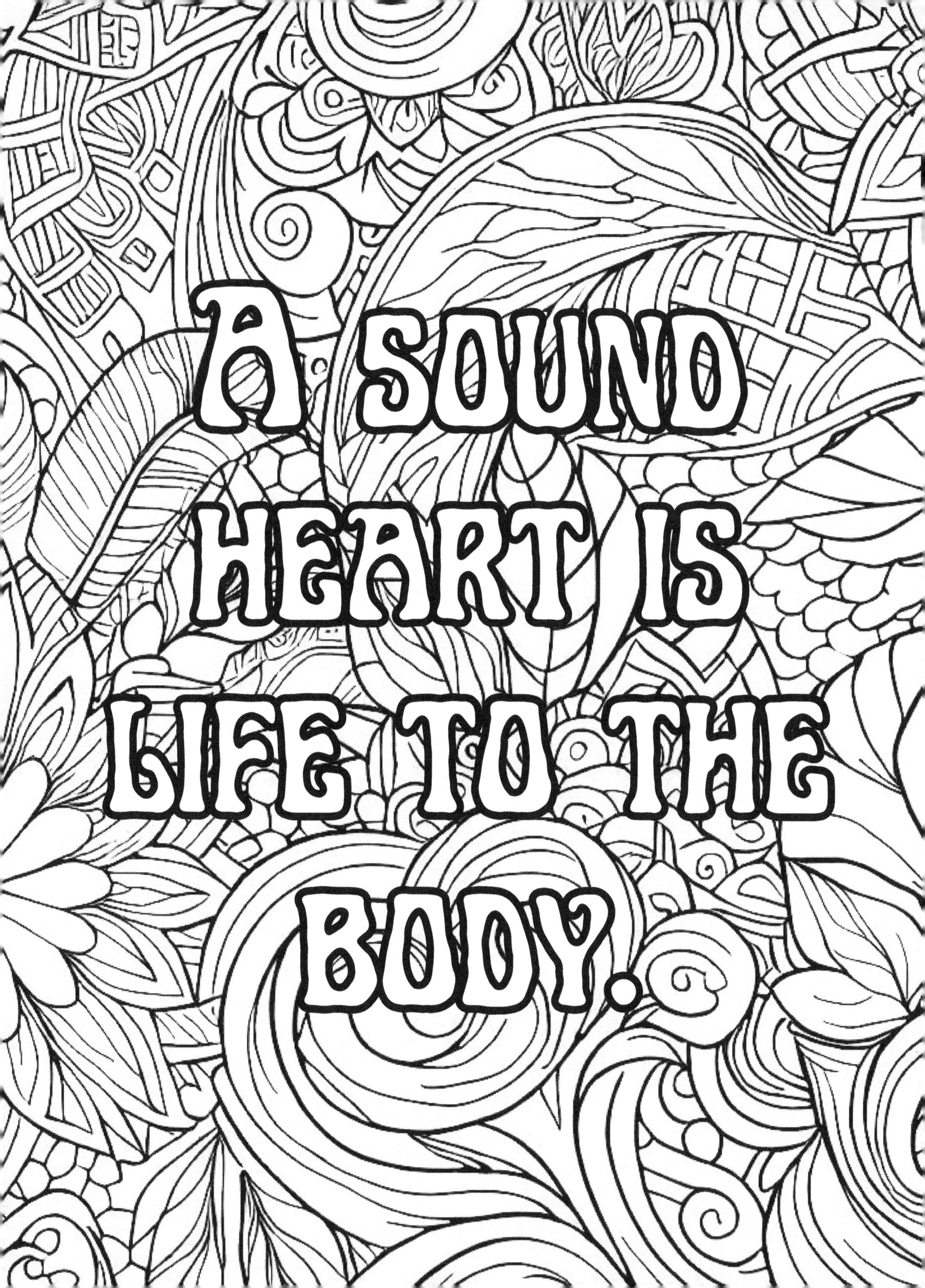
A SOUND HEART IS LIFE TO THE BODY.

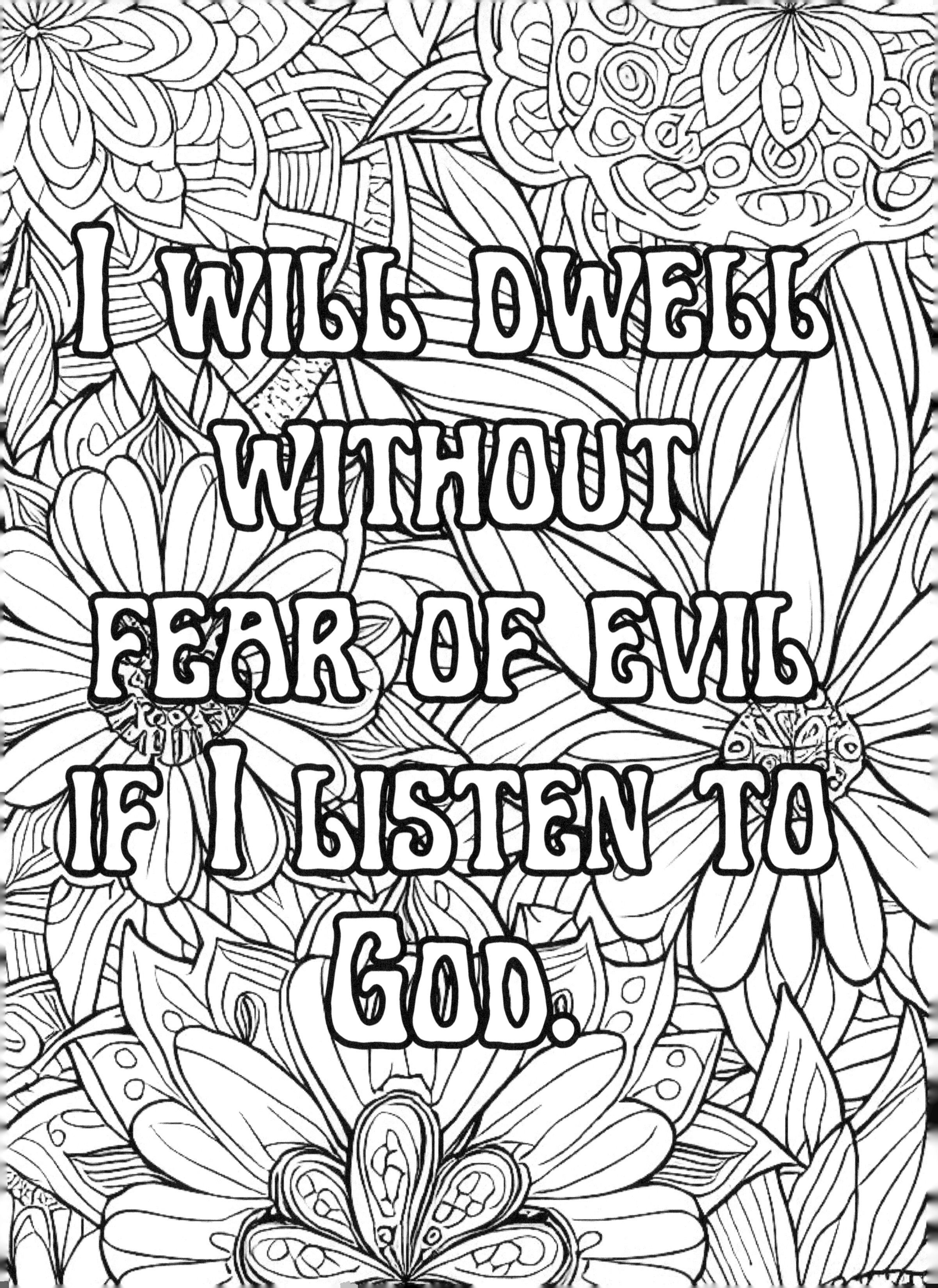
I will dwell
without
fear of evil
if I listen to
God.

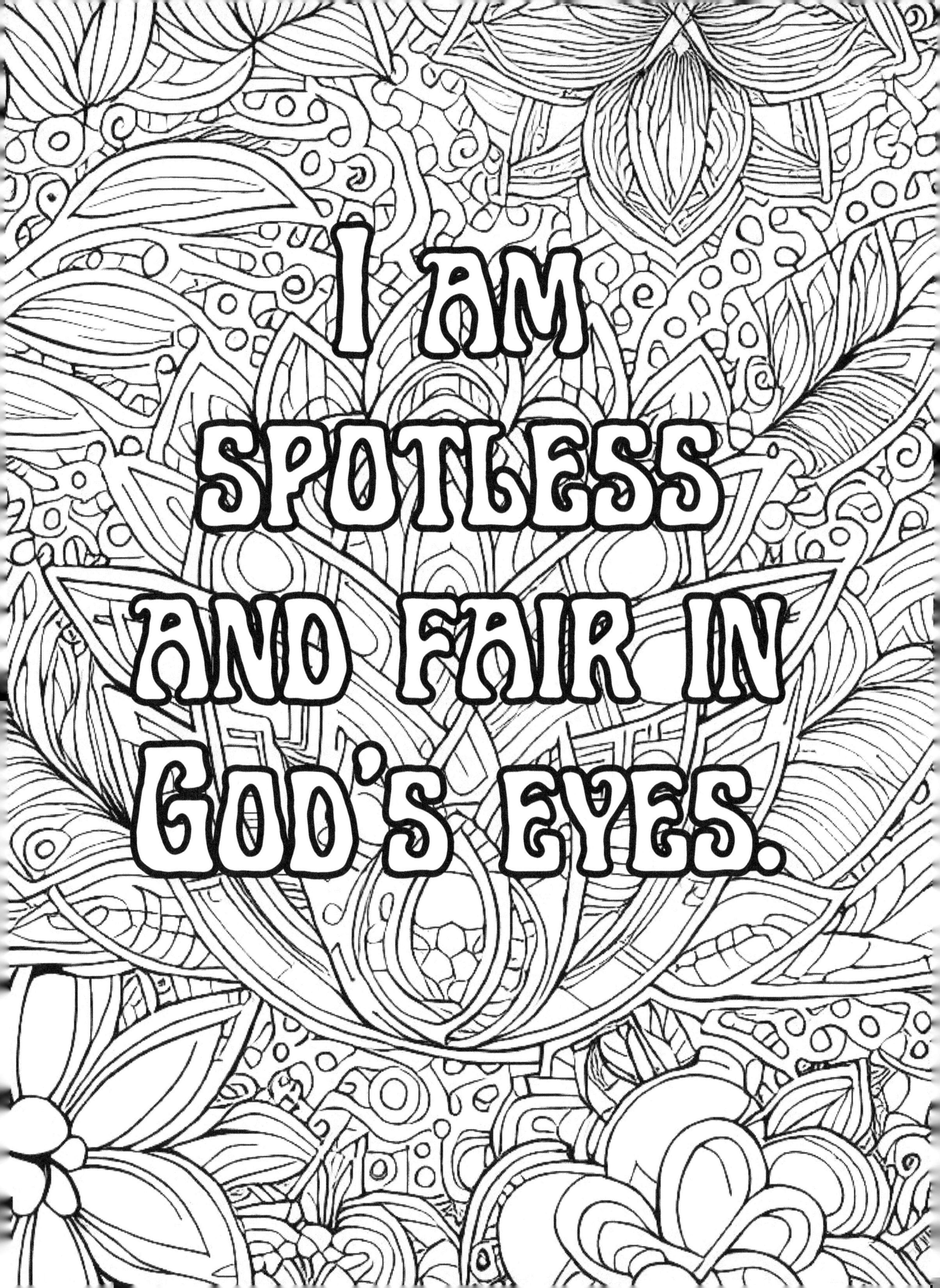
I AM
SPOTLESS
AND FAIR IN
GOD'S EYES.

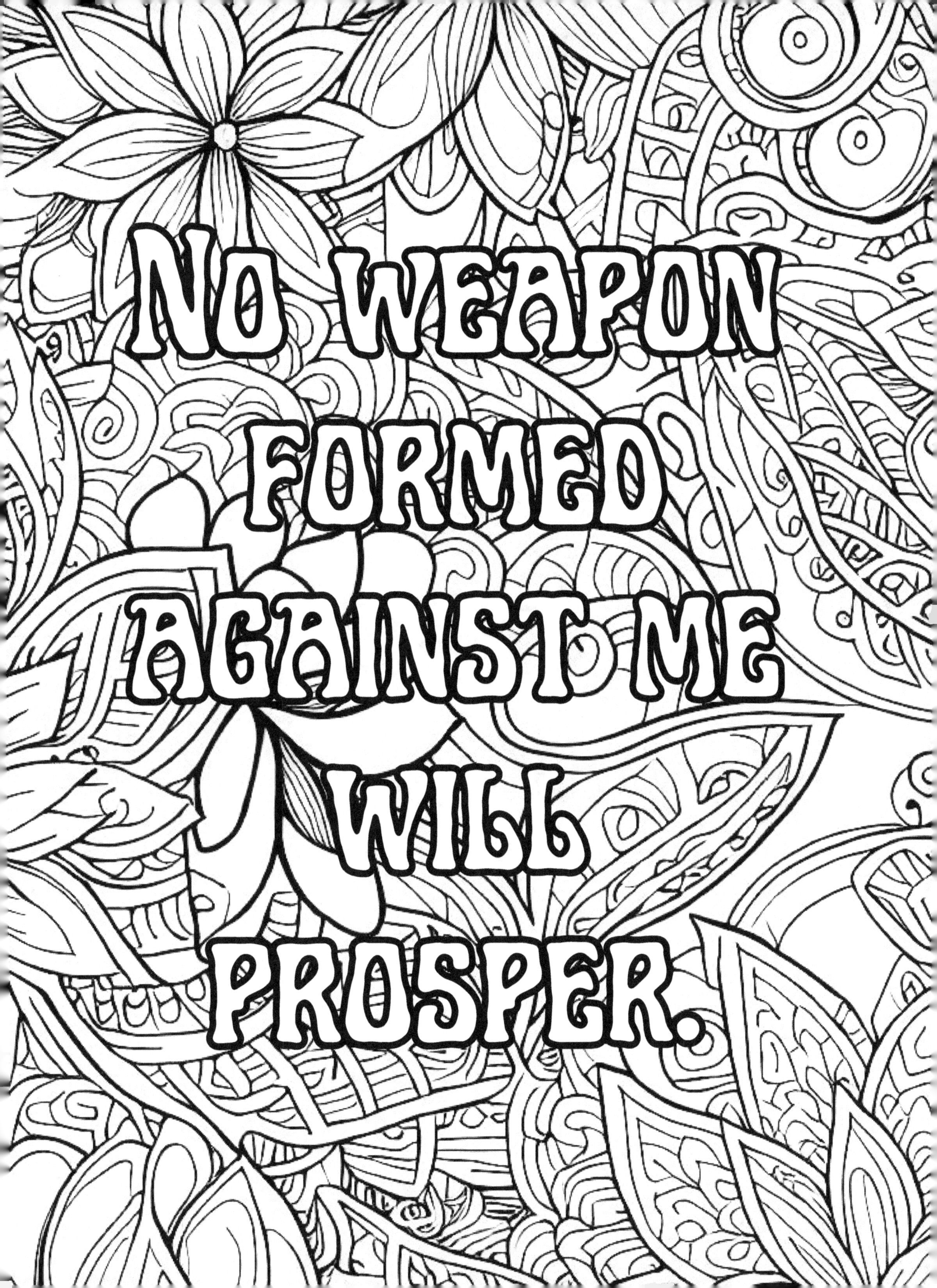
No weapon
formed
against me
will
prosper.

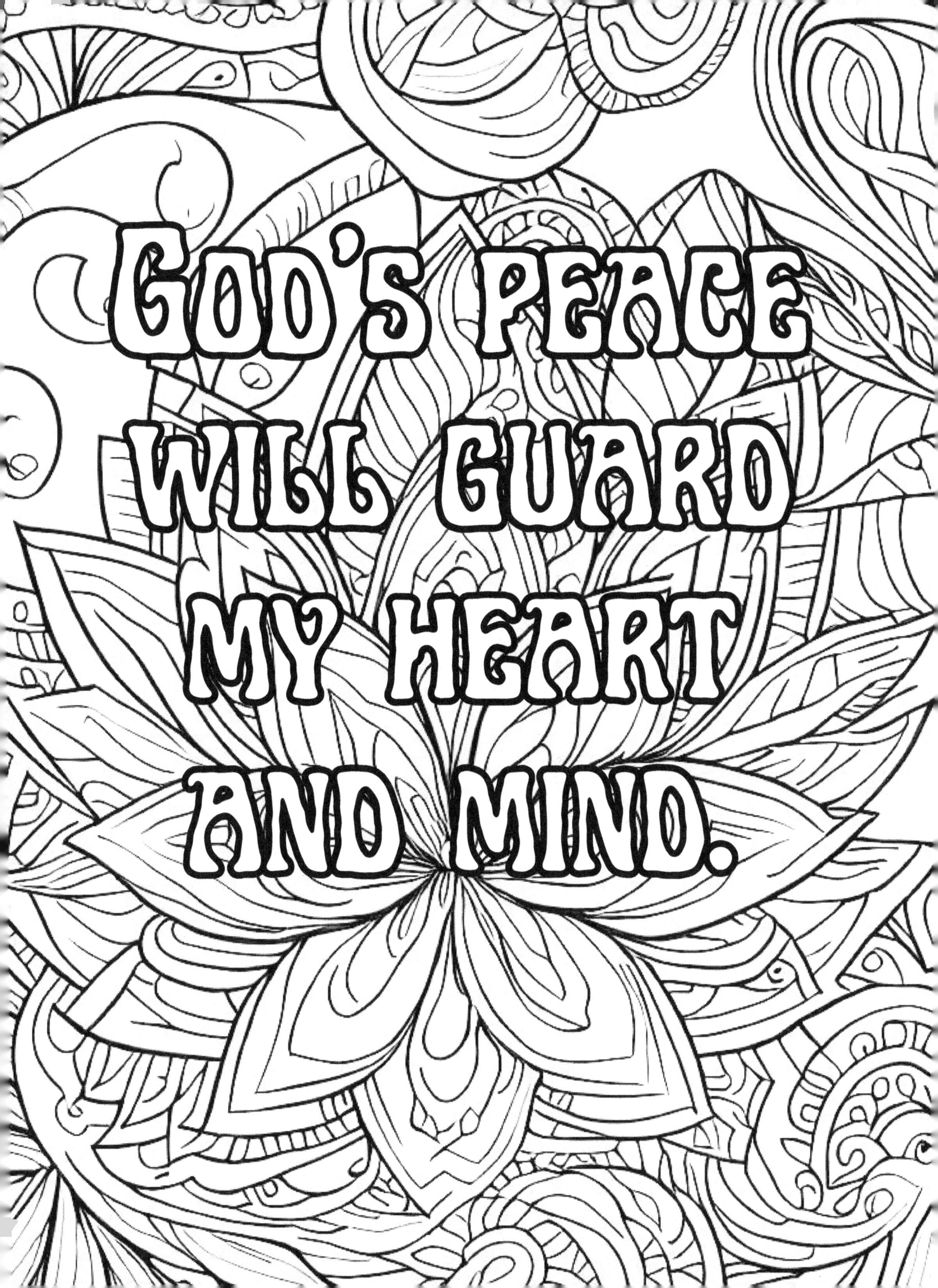
GOD'S PEACE
WILL GUARD
MY HEART
AND MIND.

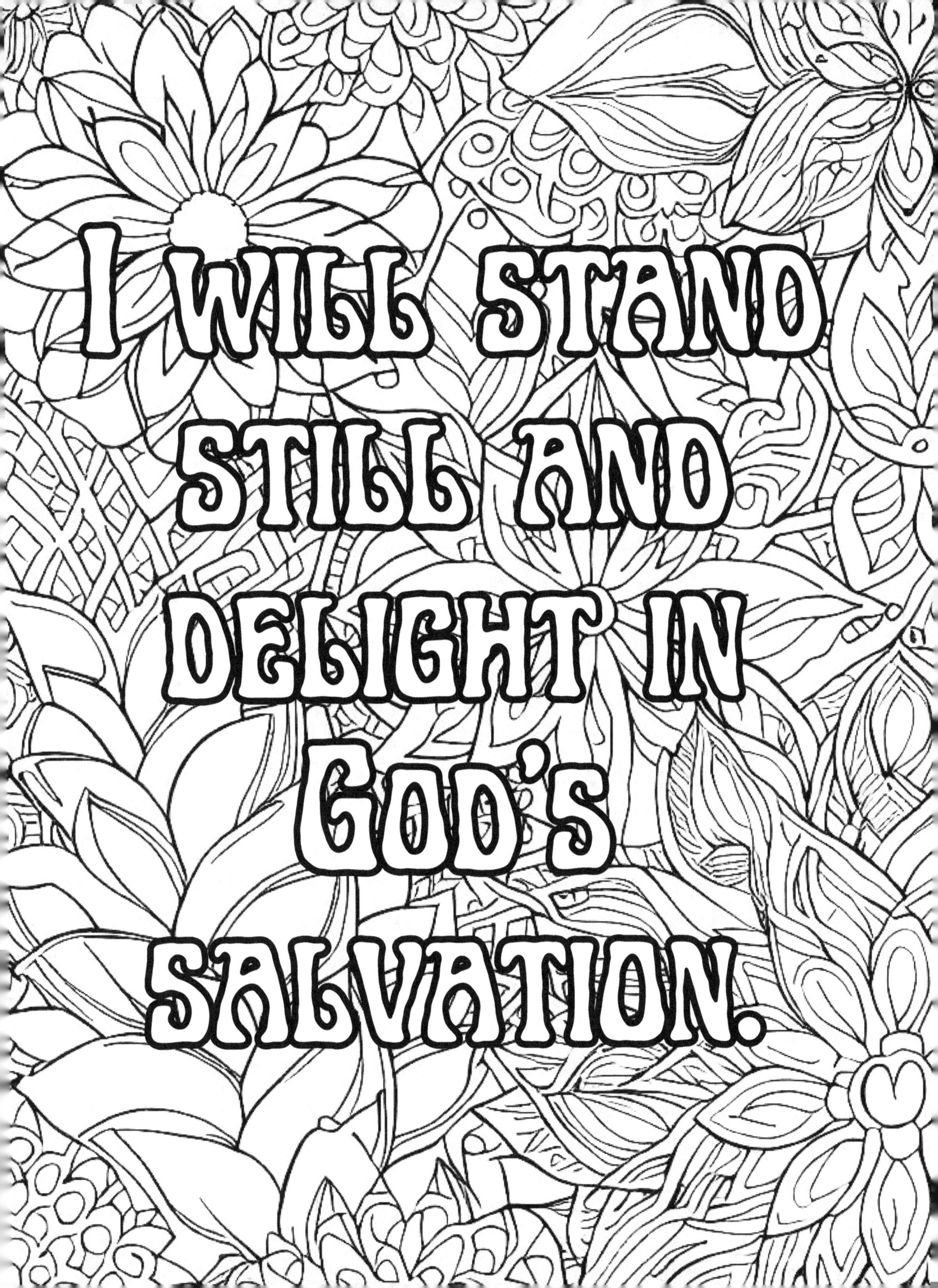
I WILL STAND
STILL AND
DELIGHT IN
GOD'S
SALVATION.

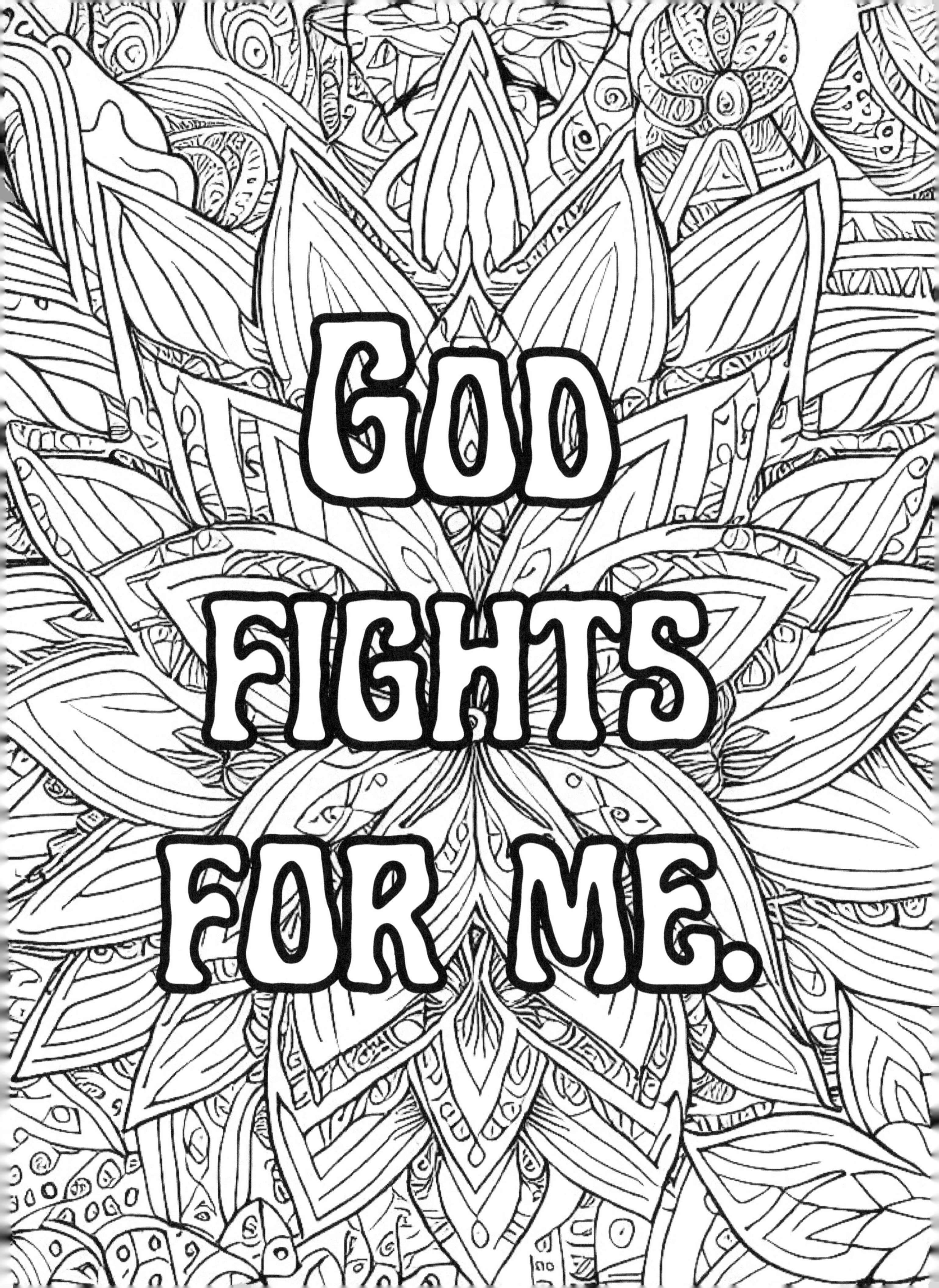
GOD
FIGHTS
FOR ME.

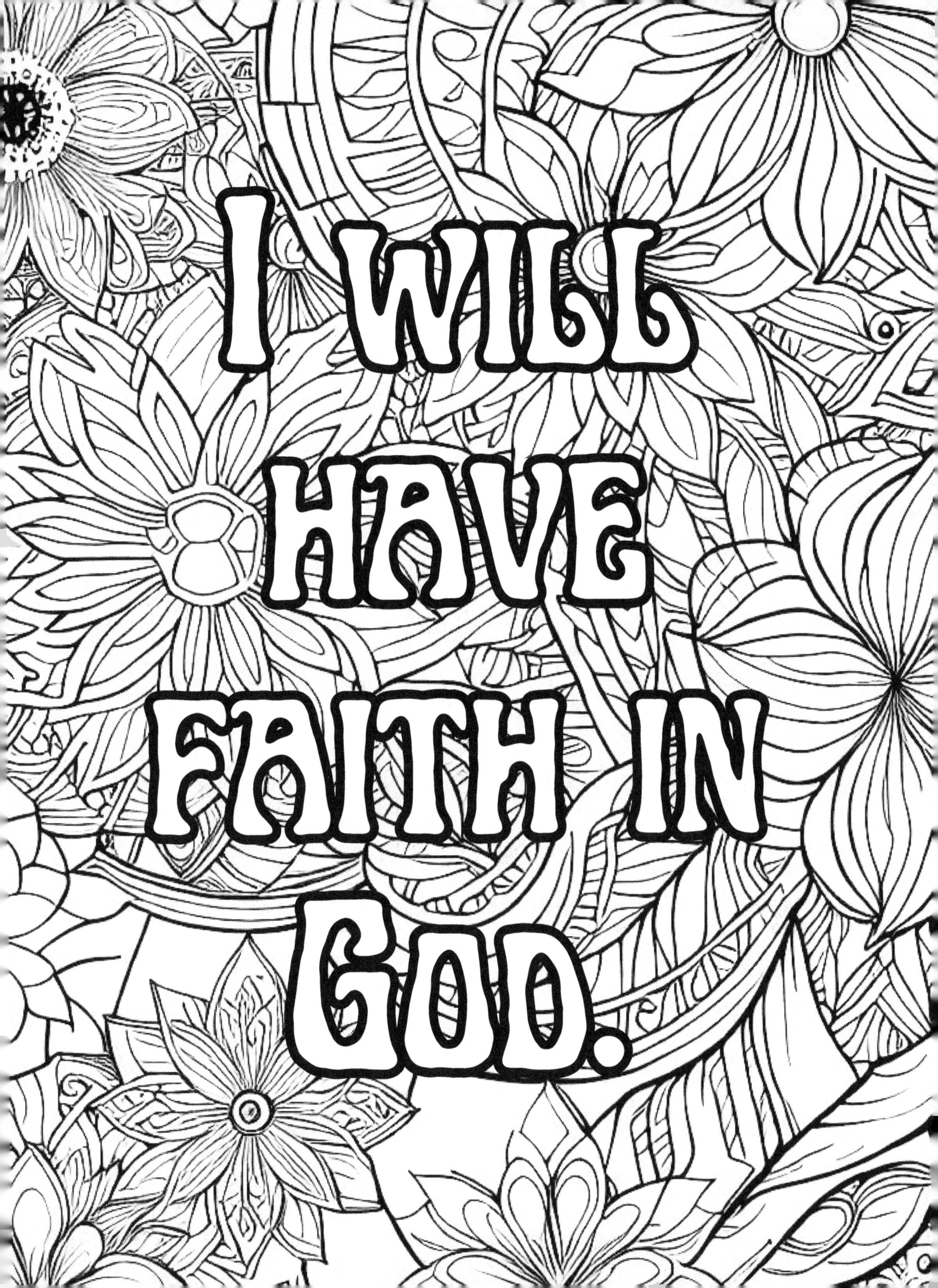
I WILL
HAVE
FAITH IN
GOD.

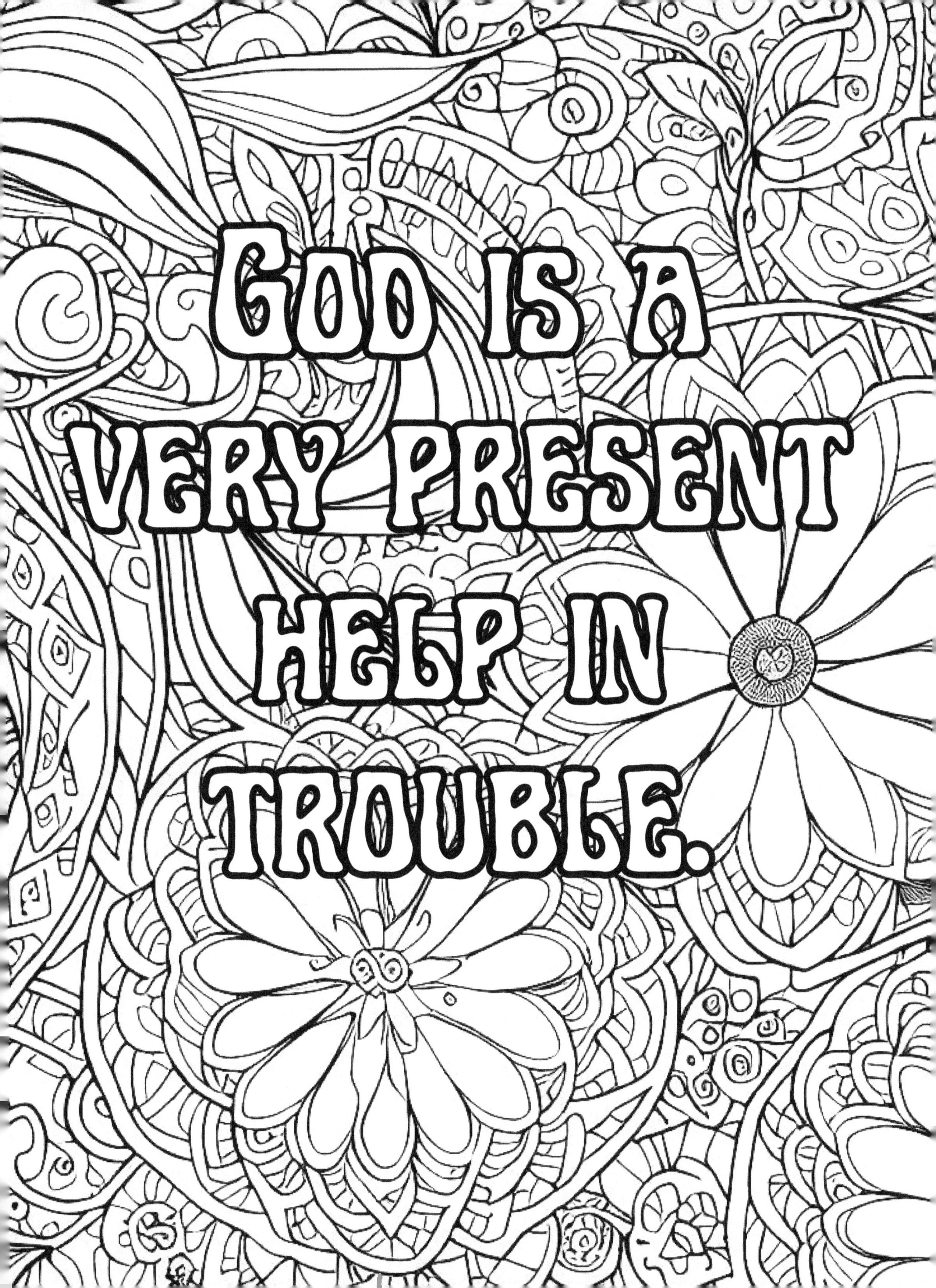
GOD IS A
VERY PRESENT
HELP IN
TROUBLE.

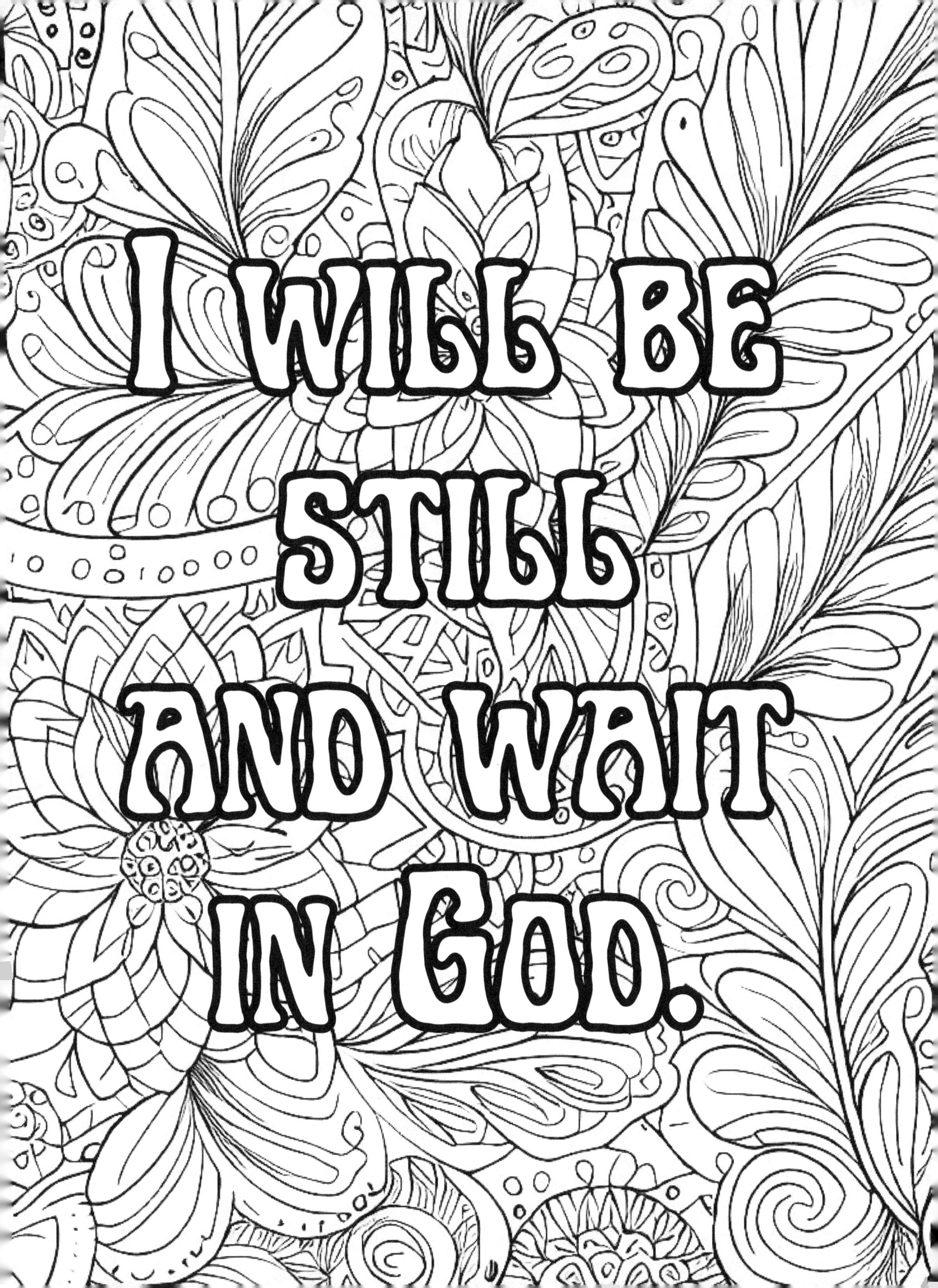
I WILL BE
STILL
AND WAIT
IN GOD.

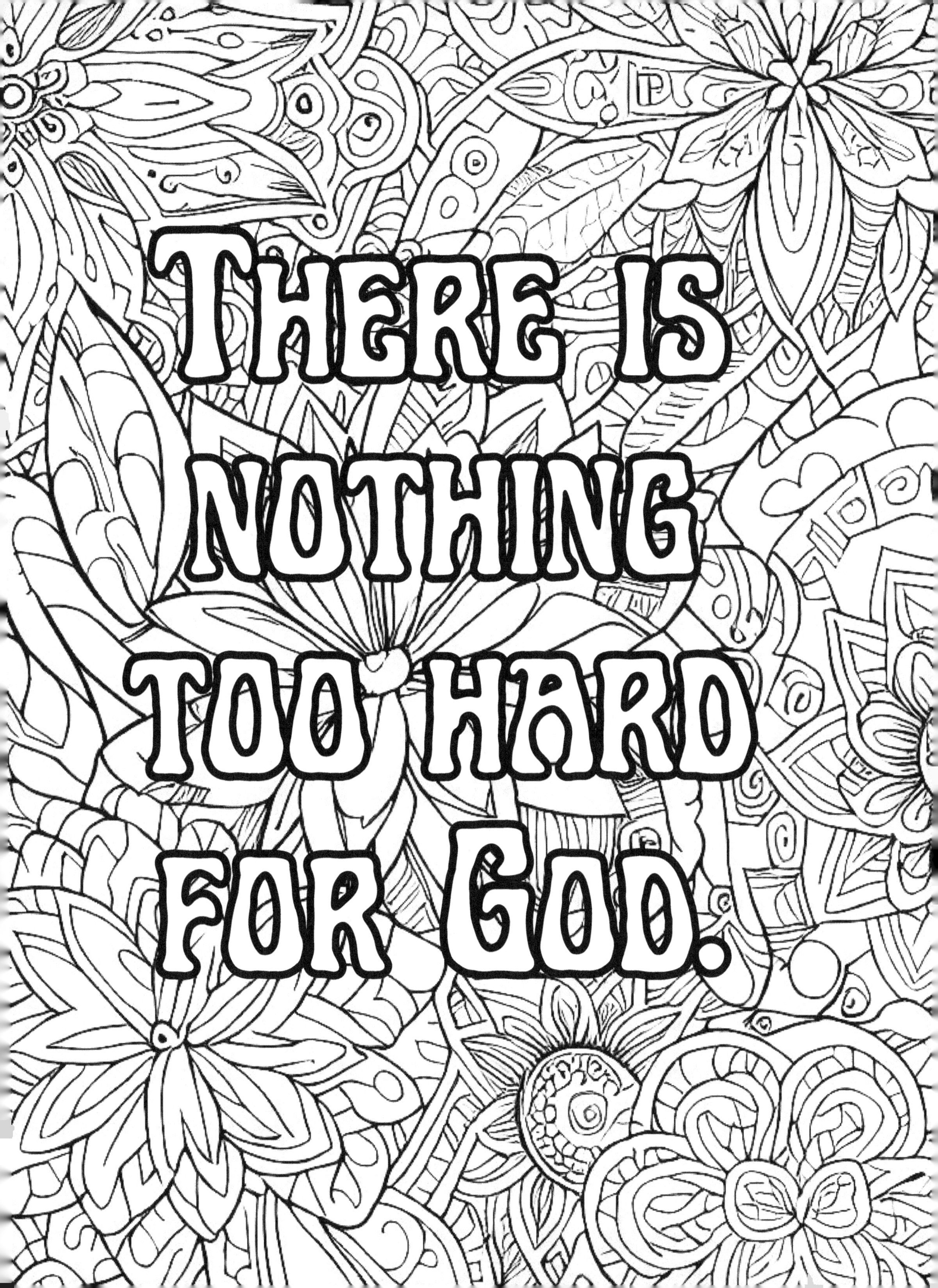
There is nothing too hard for God.

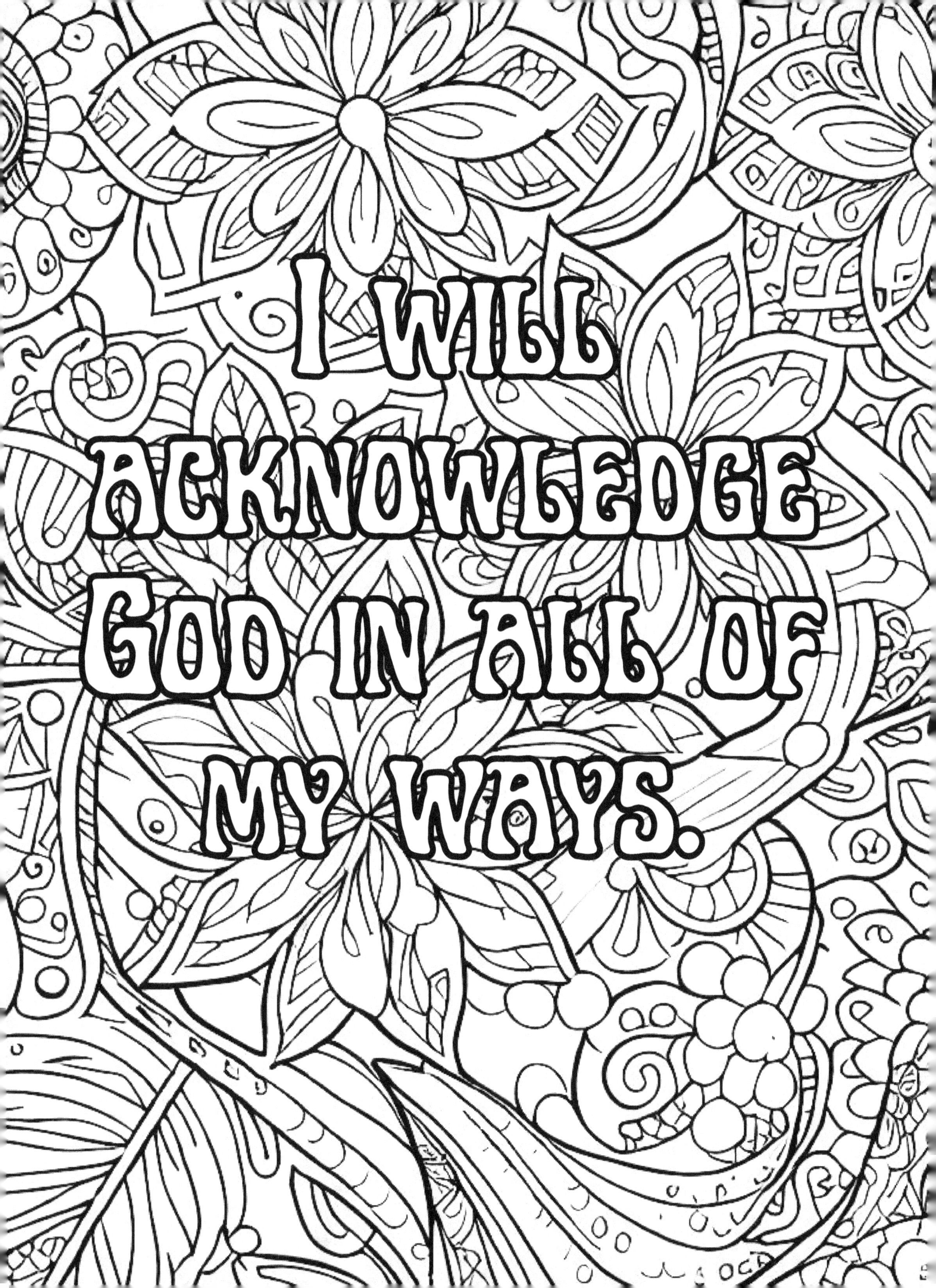
I will
acknowledge
God in all of
my ways.

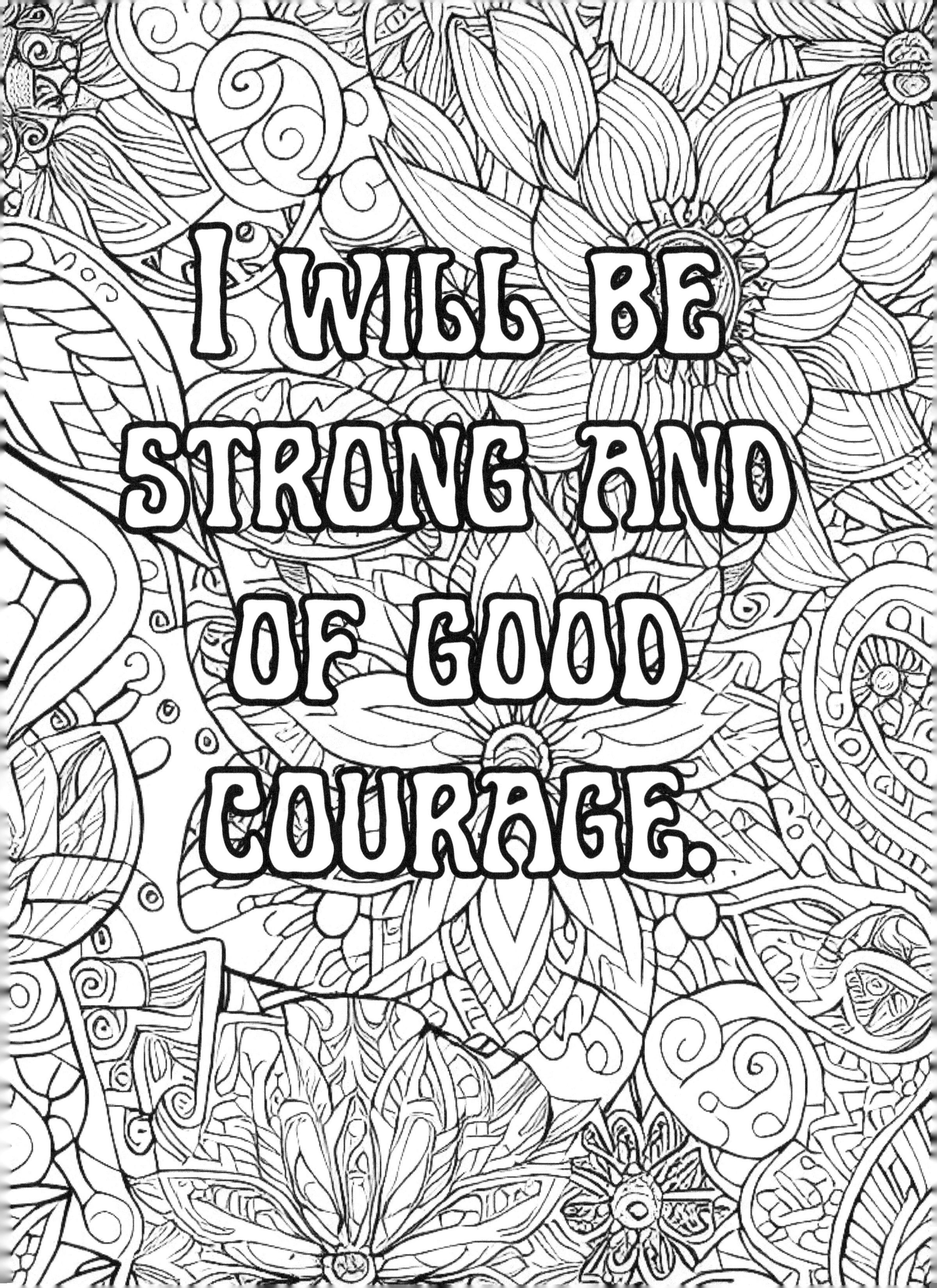
I WILL BE
STRONG AND
OF GOOD
COURAGE.

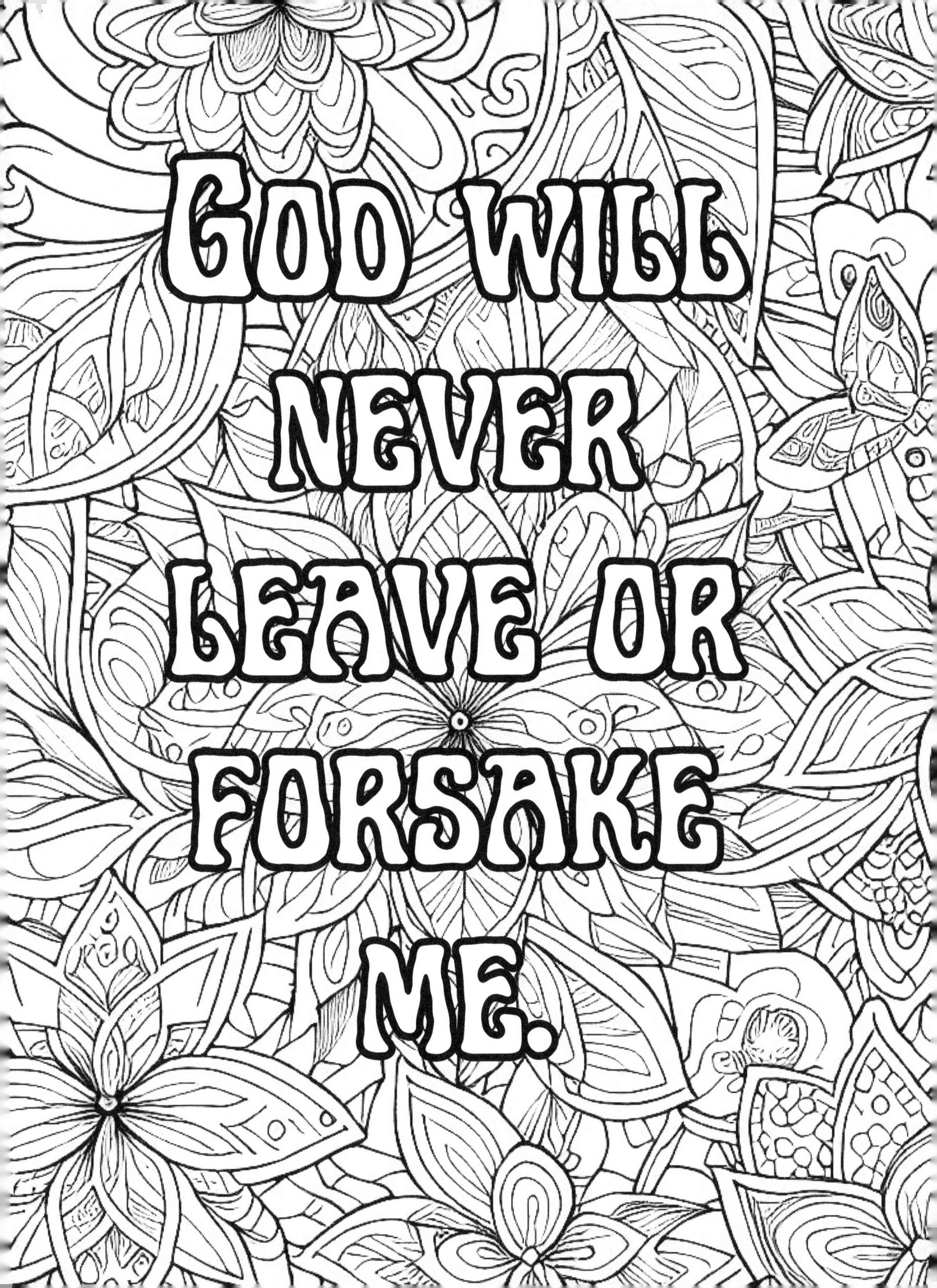
GOD WILL
NEVER
LEAVE OR
FORSAKE
ME.

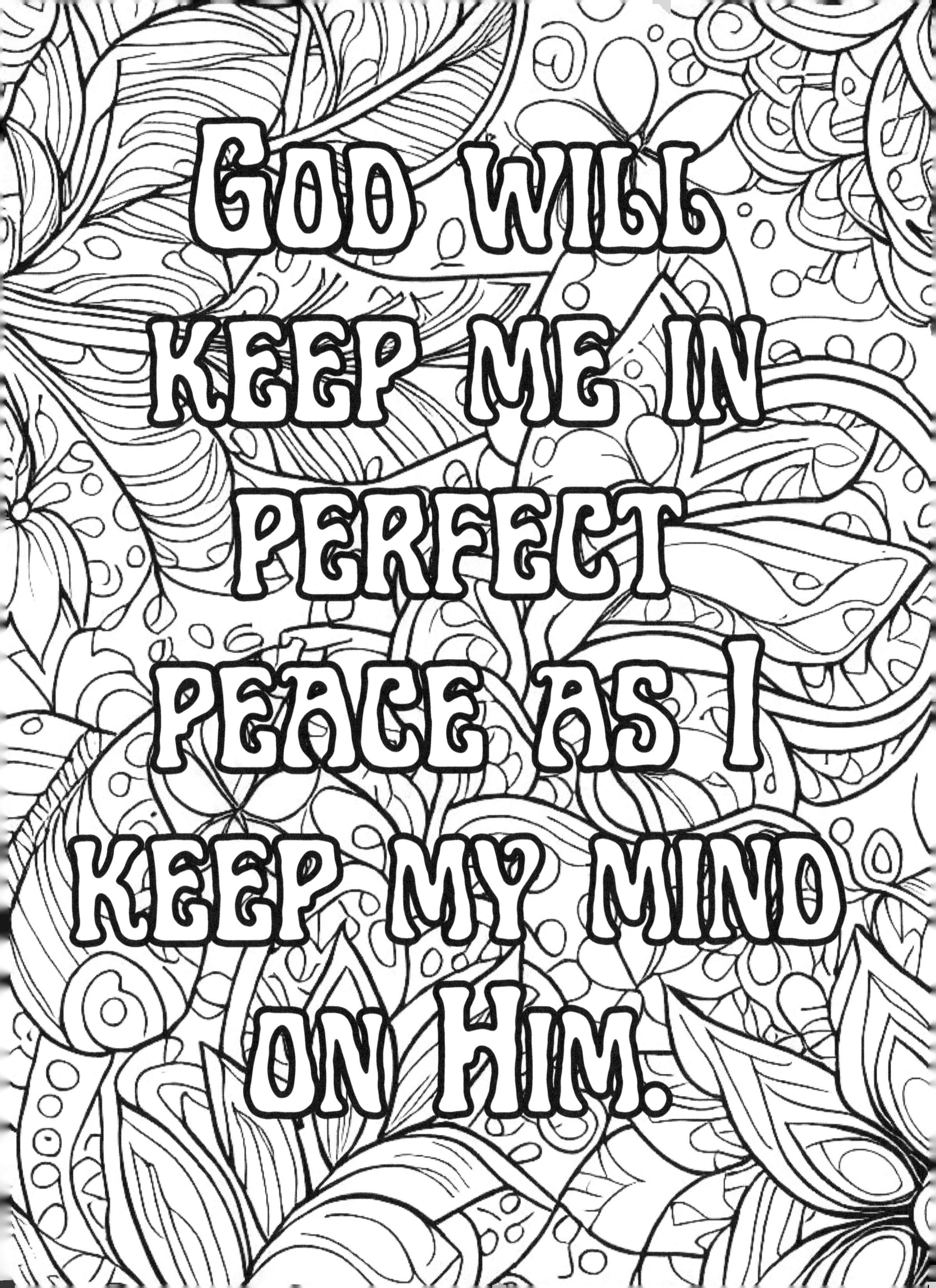
God will keep me in perfect peace as I keep my mind on Him.

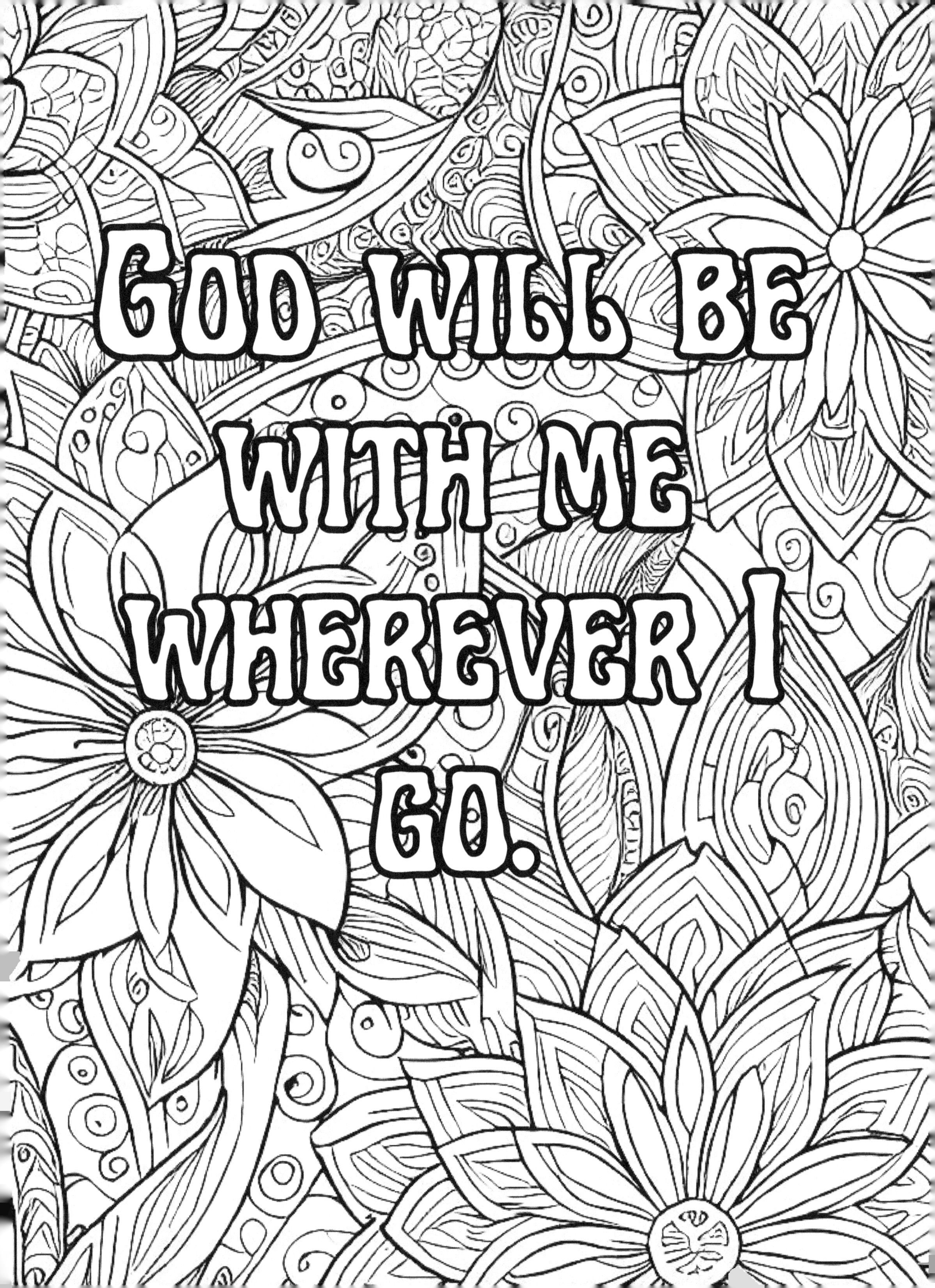
GOD WILL BE
WITH ME
WHEREVER I
GO.

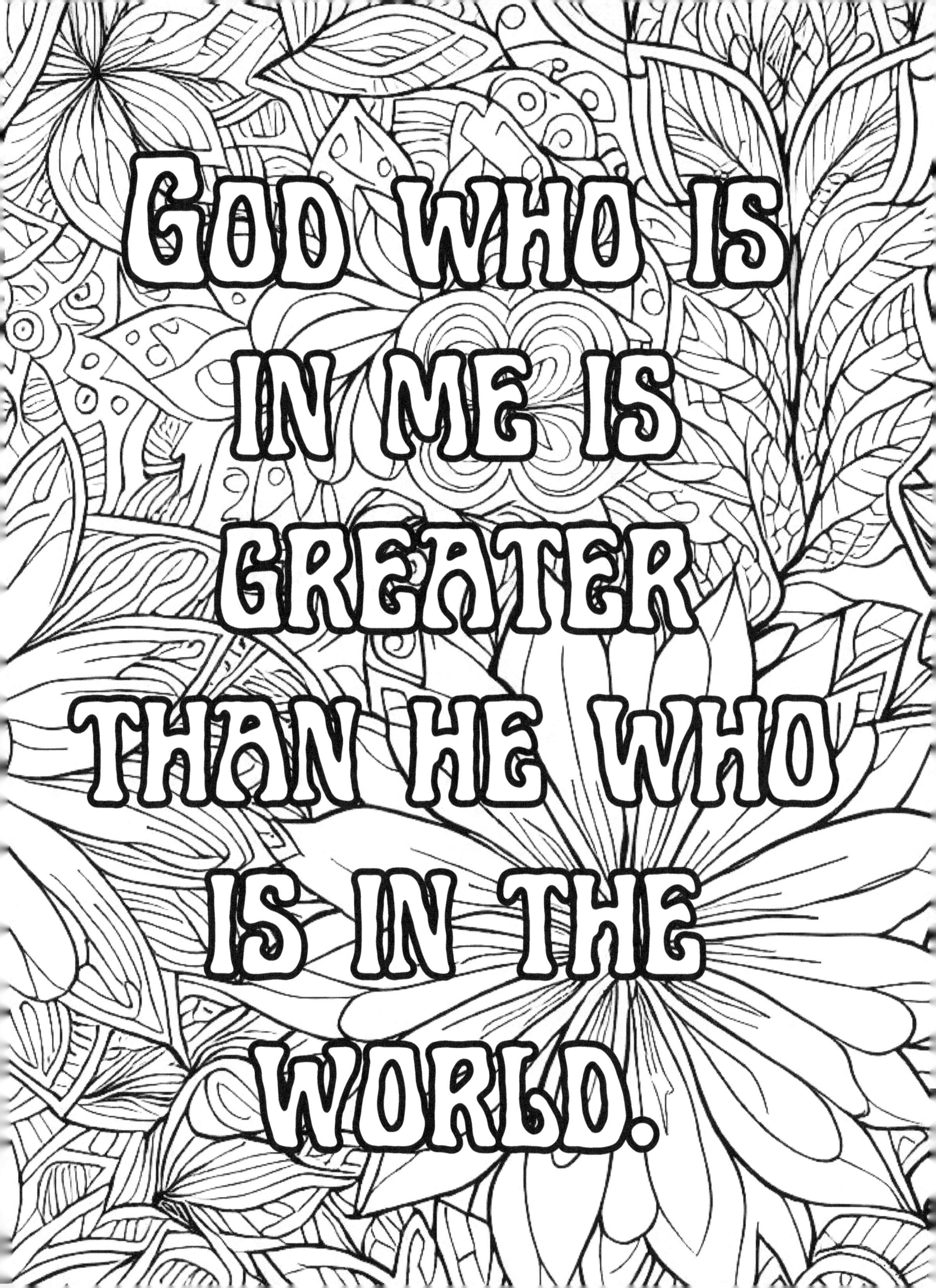
GOD WHO IS
IN ME IS
GREATER
THAN HE WHO
IS IN THE
WORLD.

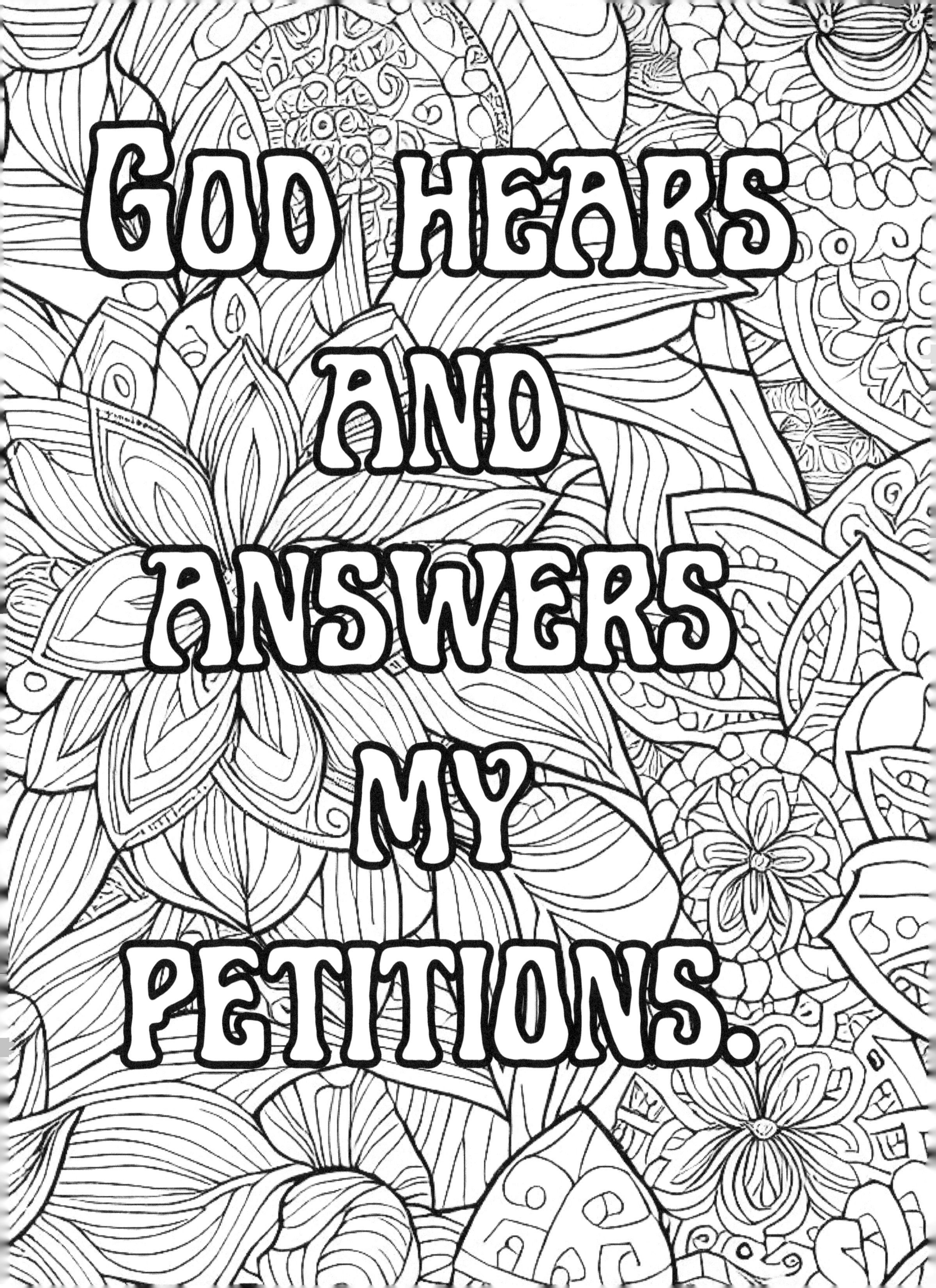
GOD HEARS
AND
ANSWERS
MY
PETITIONS.

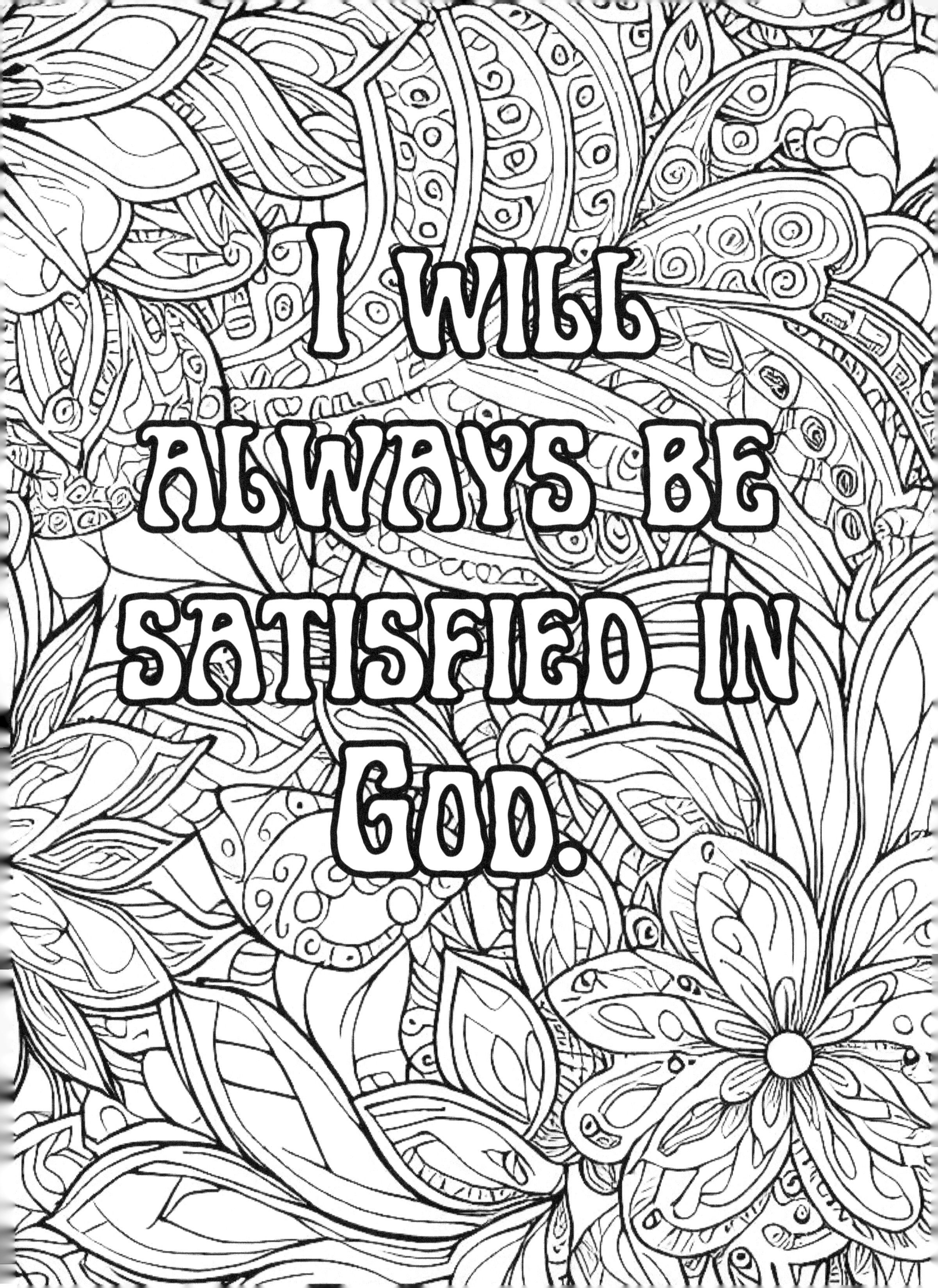
I WILL
ALWAYS BE
SATISFIED IN
GOD.

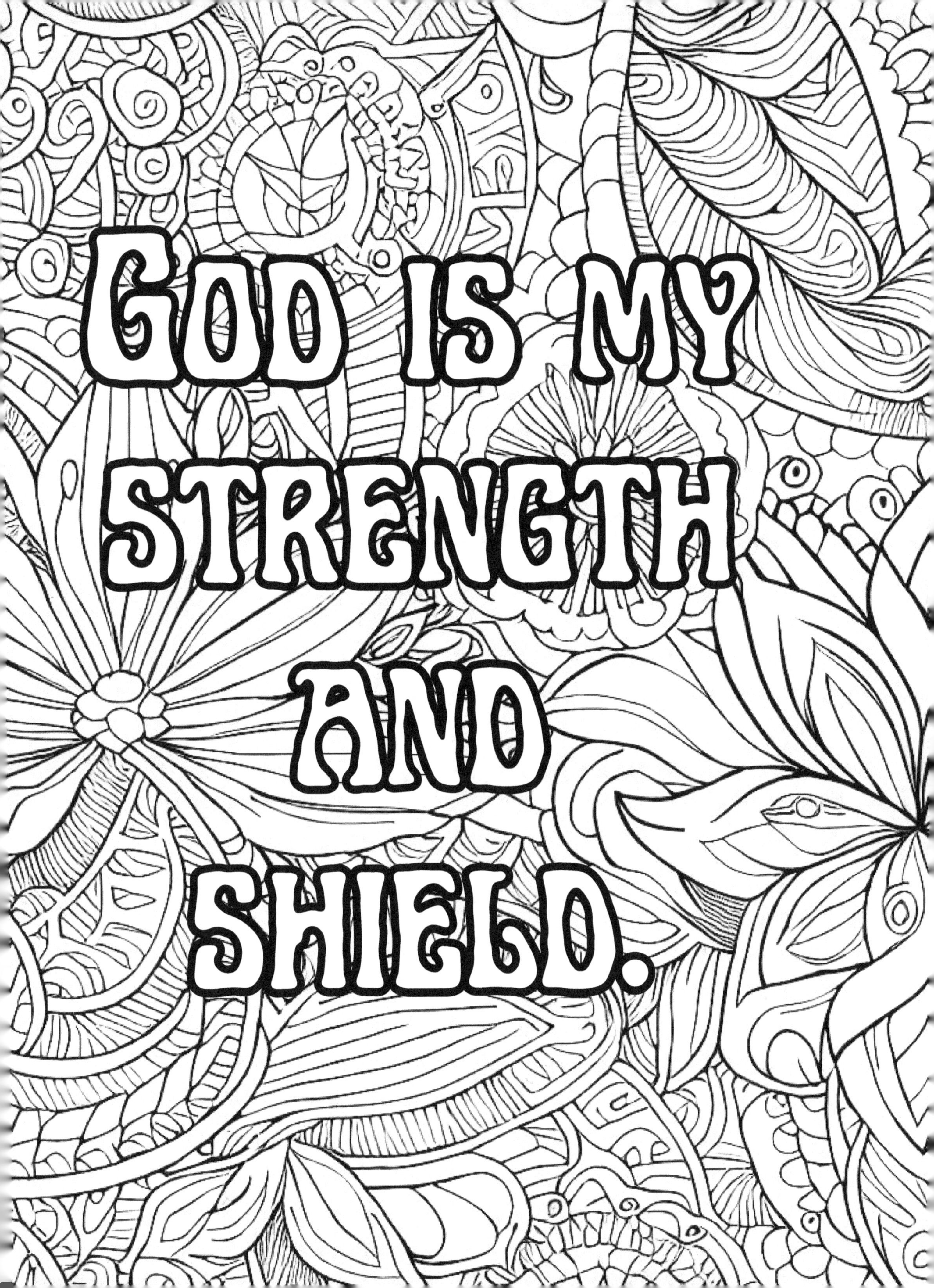
GOD IS MY
STRENGTH
AND
SHIELD.

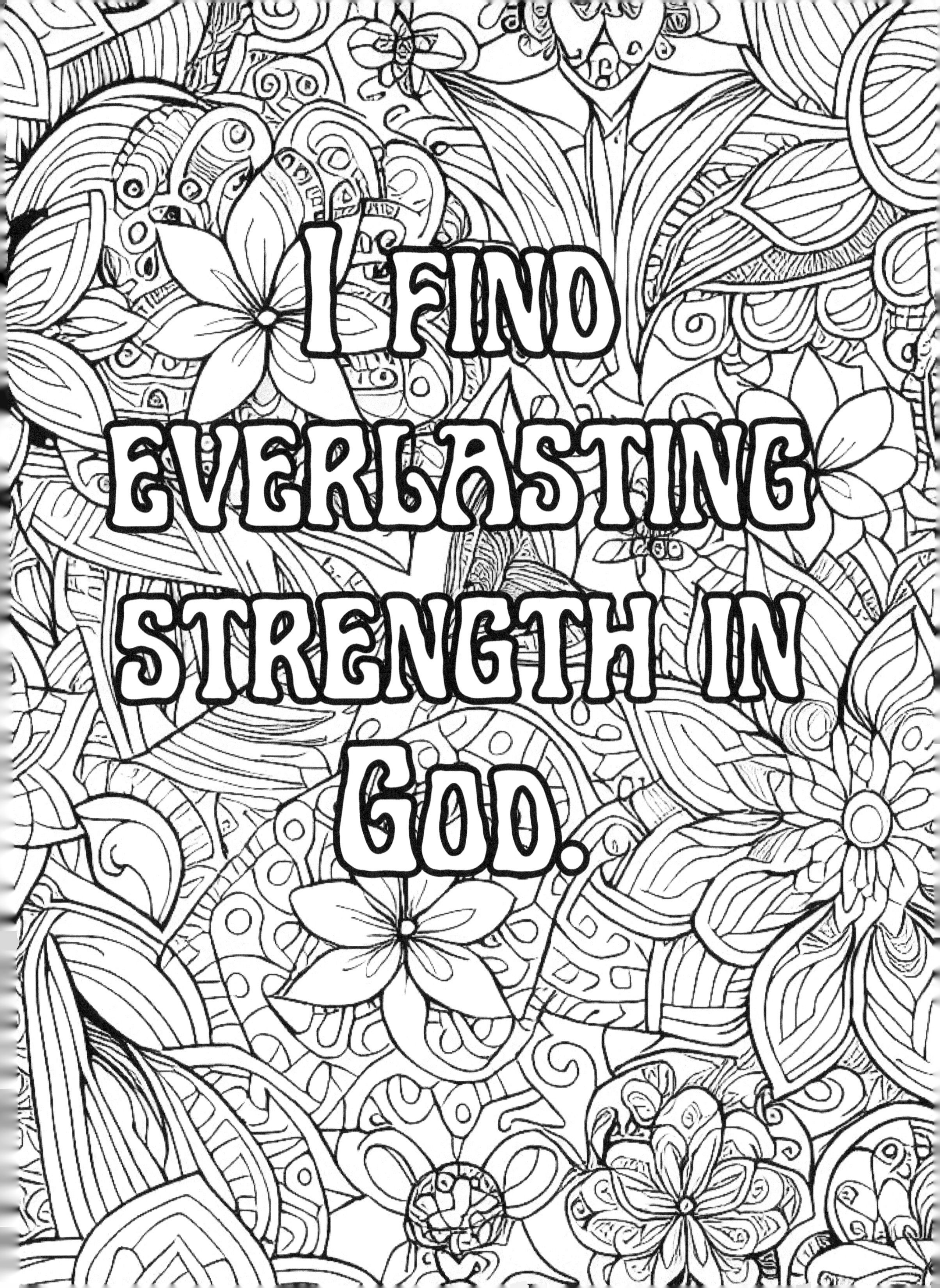
I find everlasting strength in God.

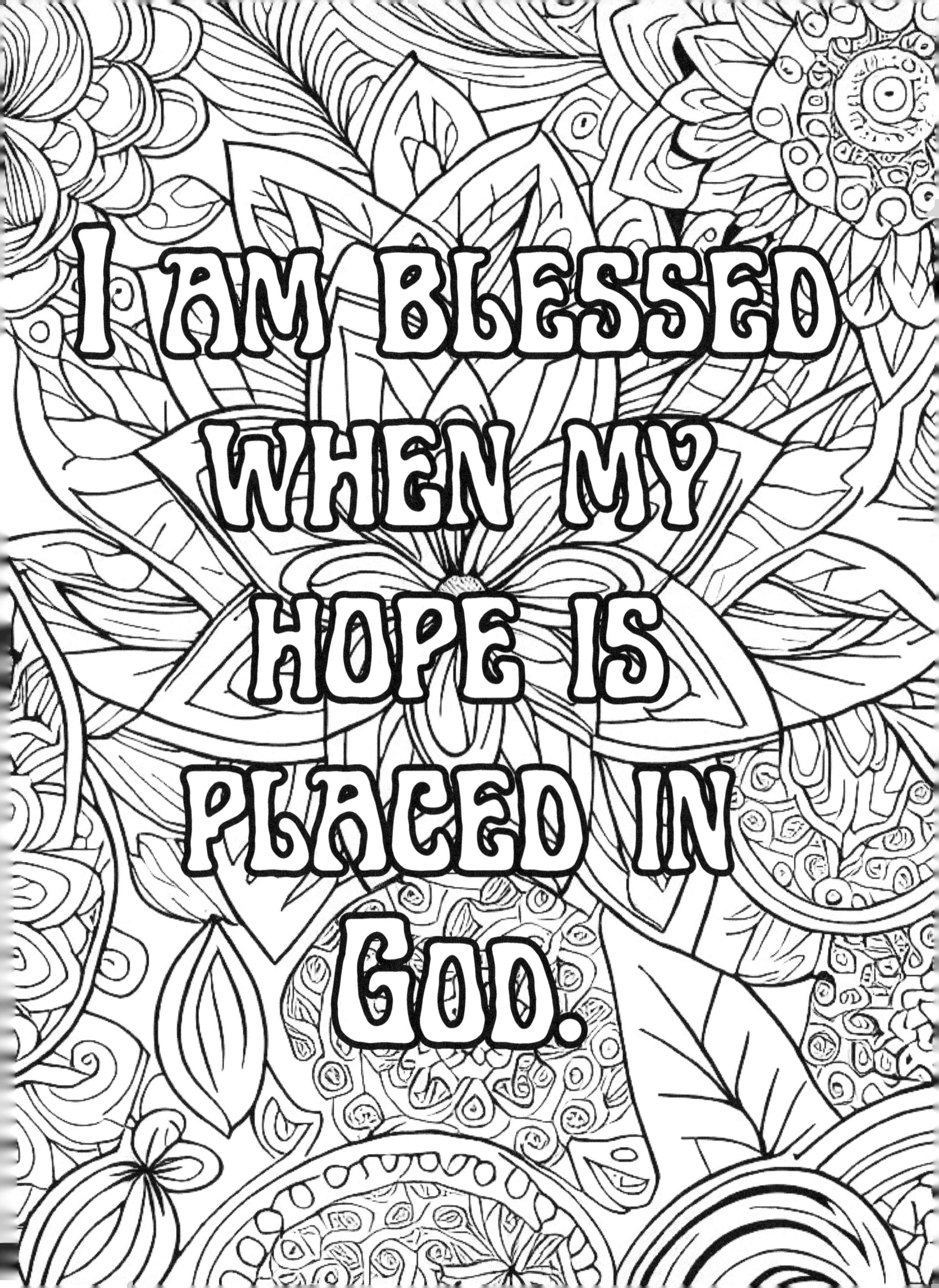
I AM BLESSED
WHEN MY
HOPE IS
PLACED IN
GOD.

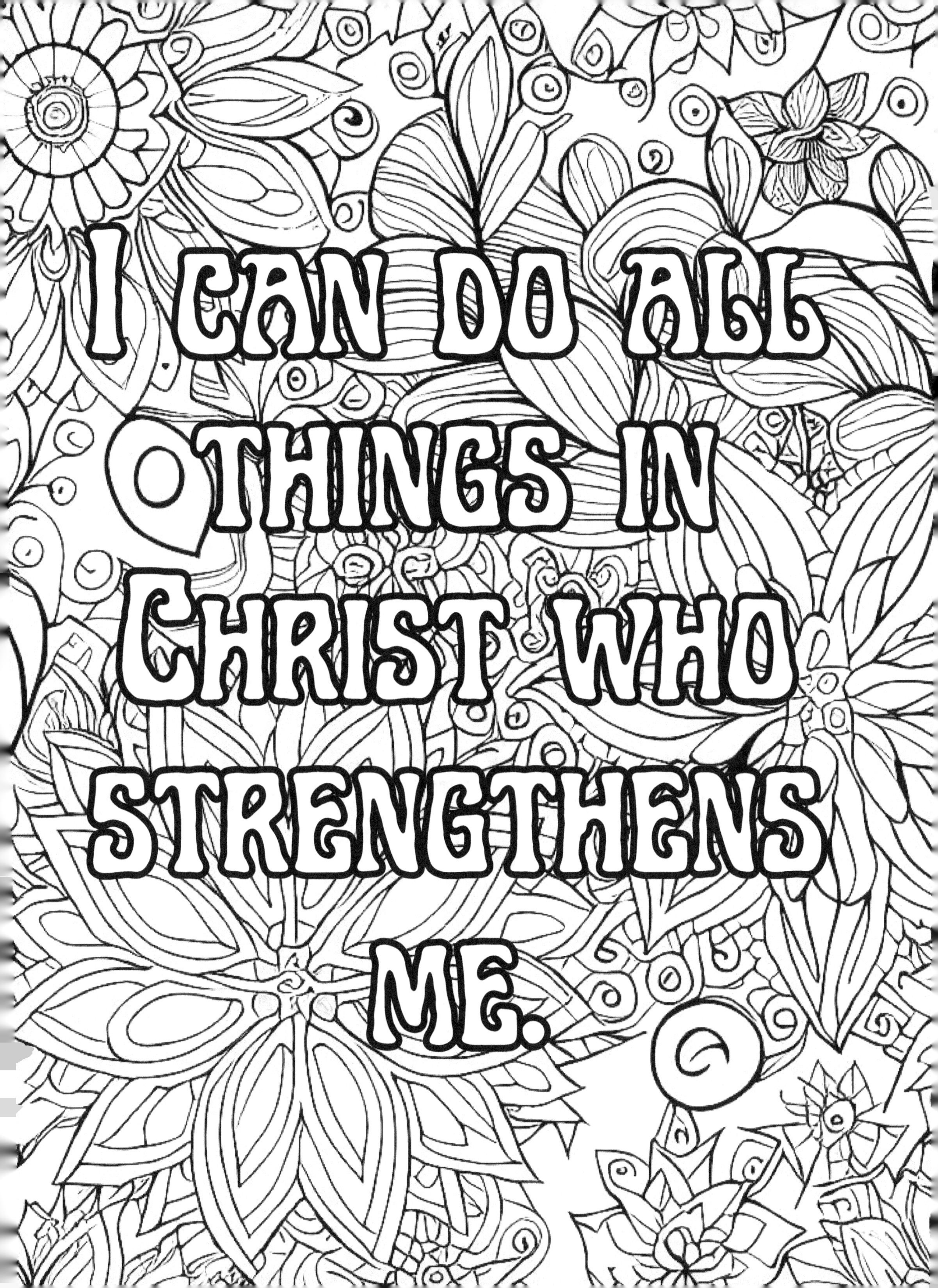
I can do all things in Christ who strengthens me.

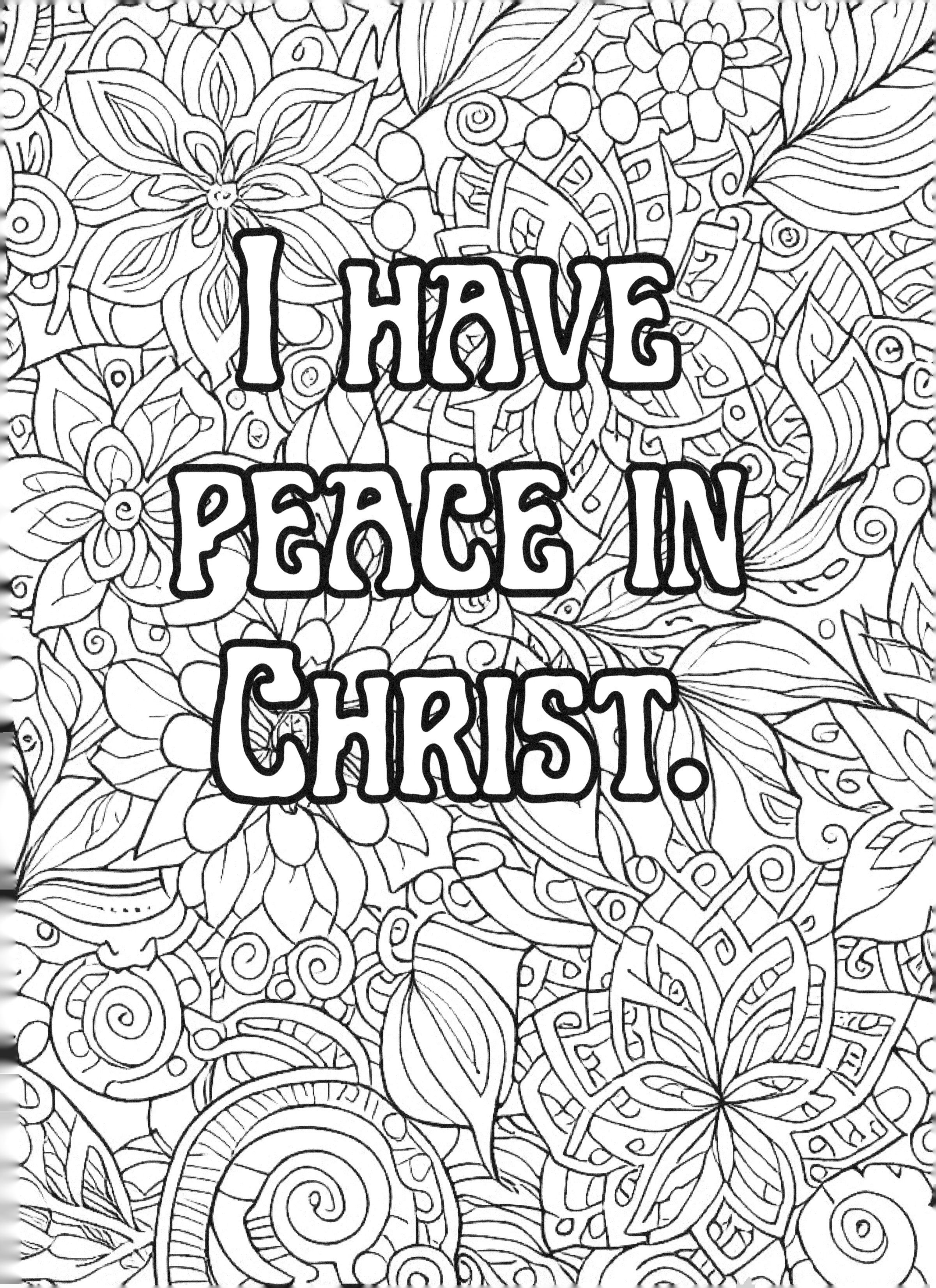
I HAVE
PEACE IN
CHRIST.

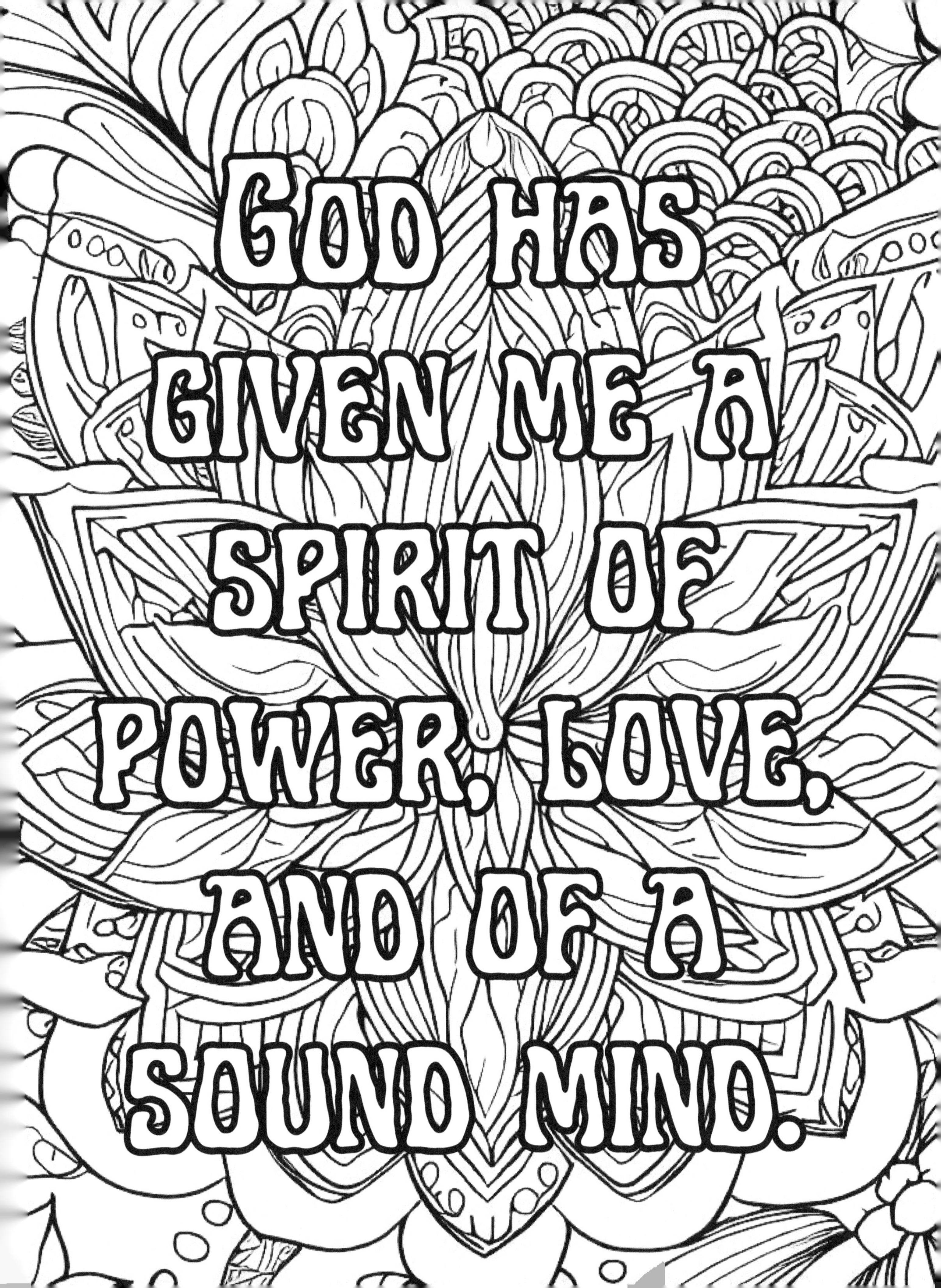
GOD HAS
GIVEN ME A
SPIRIT OF
POWER, LOVE,
AND OF A
SOUND MIND.

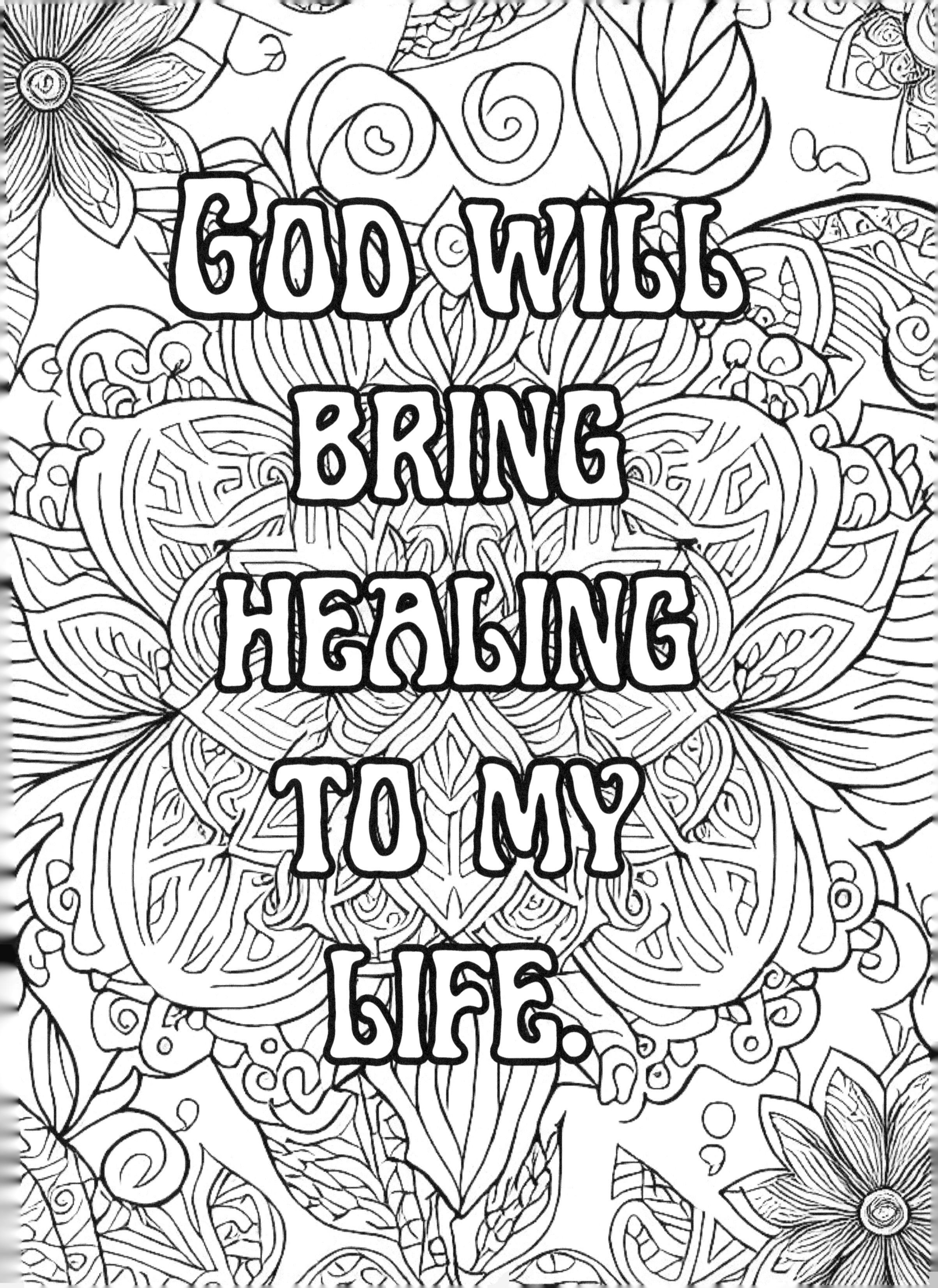
GOD WILL
BRING
HEALING
TO MY
LIFE.

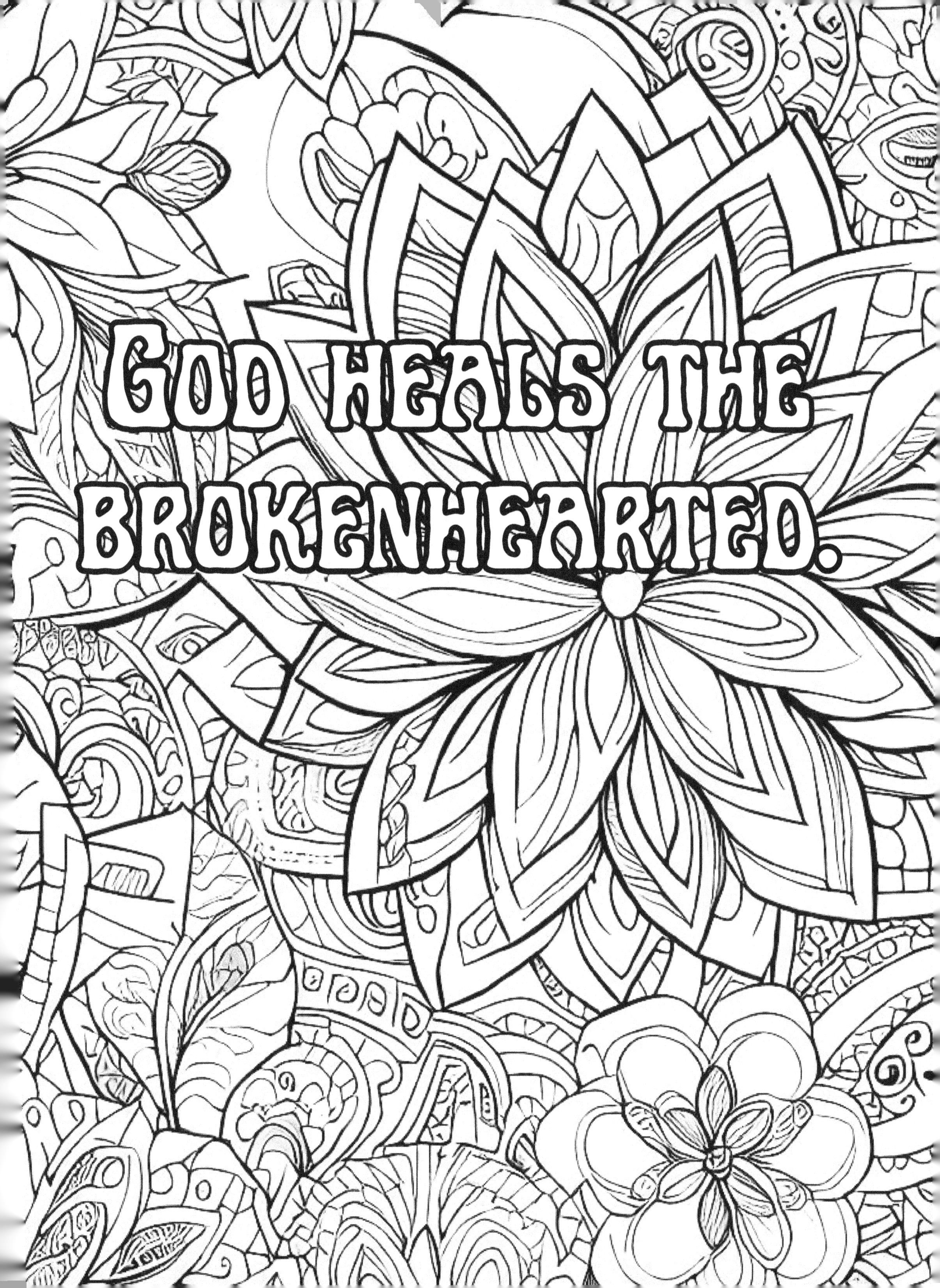
God heals the brokenhearted.

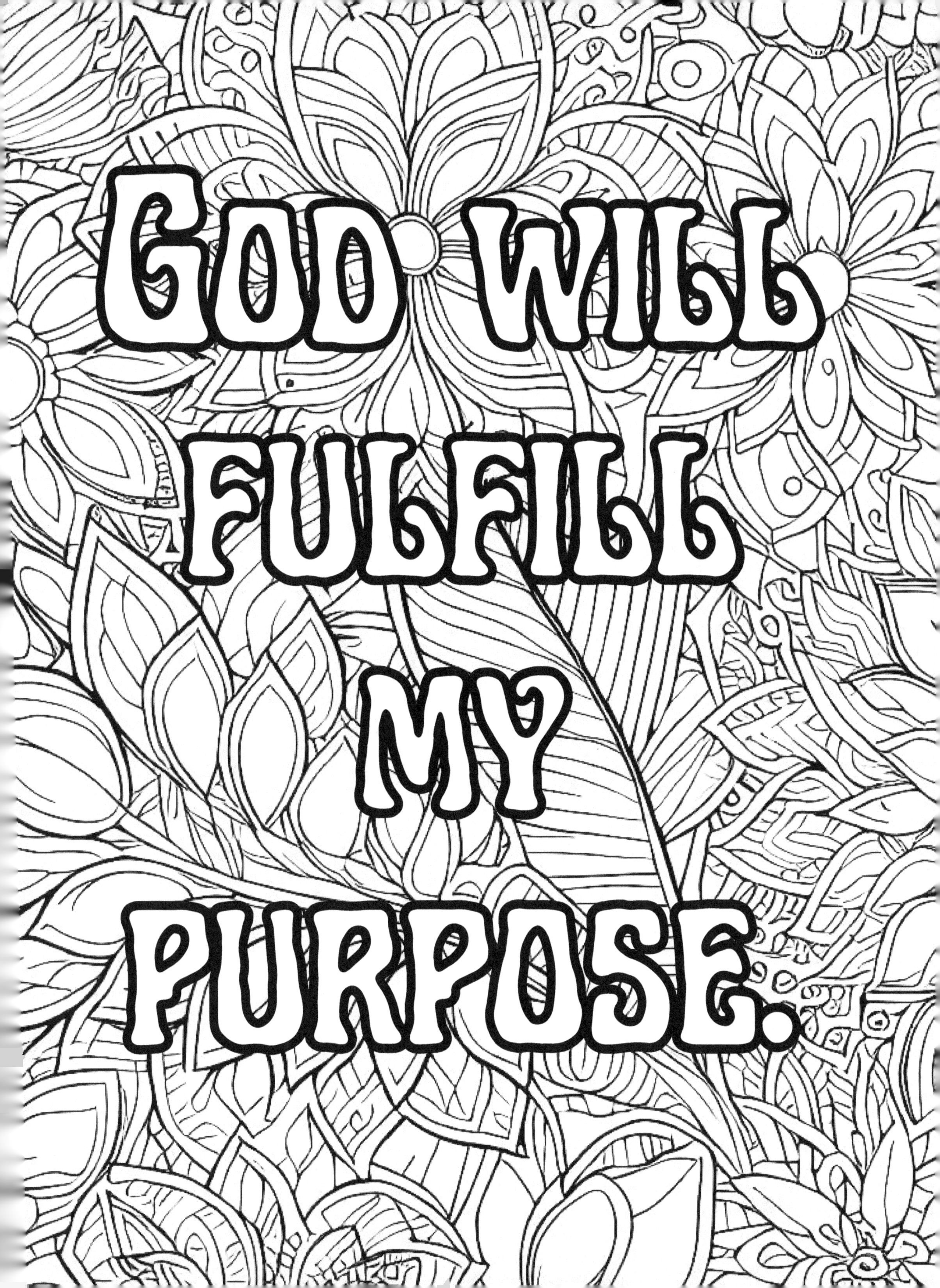
GOD WILL
FULFILL
MY
PURPOSE.

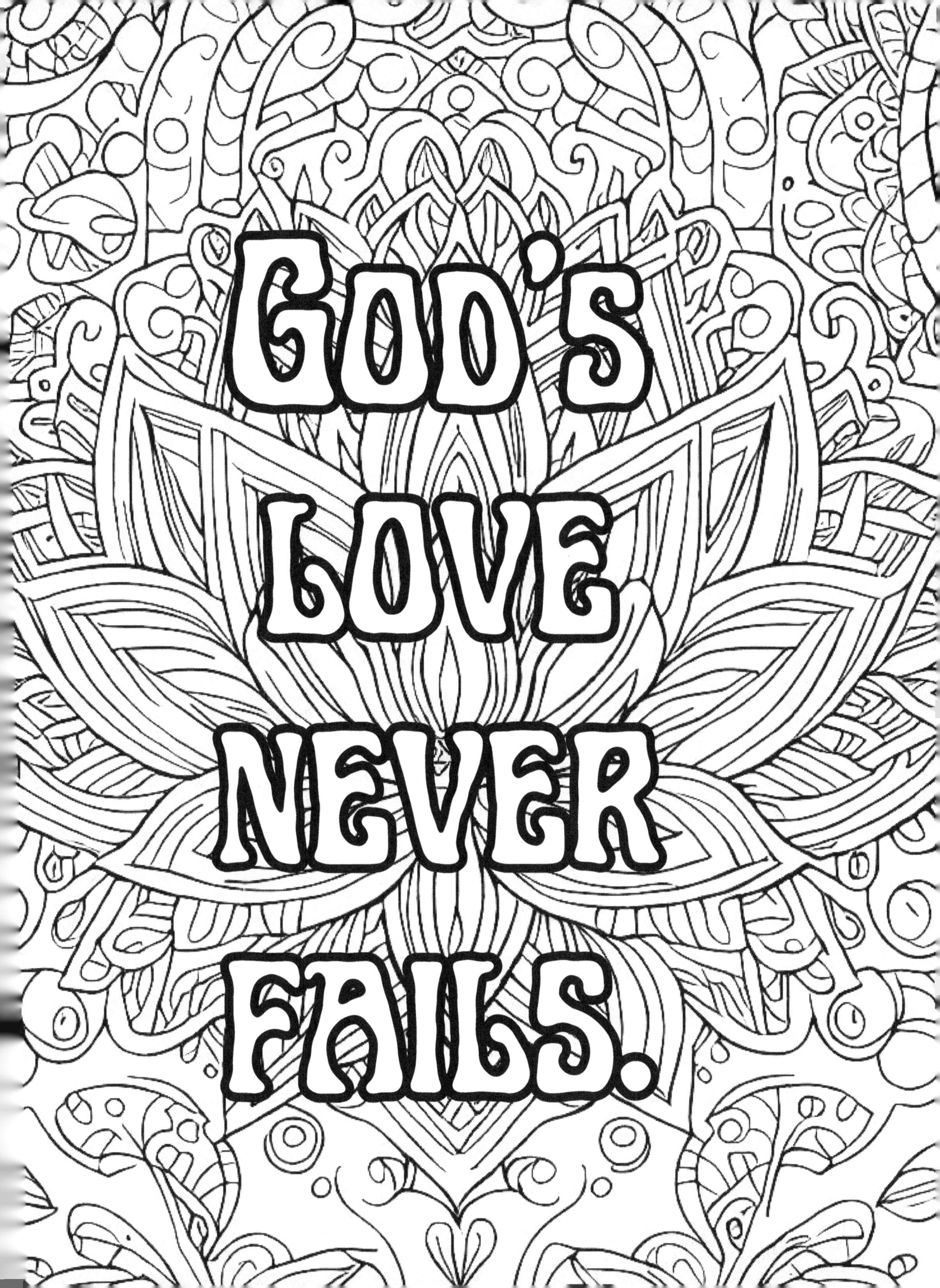
GOD'S
LOVE
NEVER
FAILS.

www.ingramcontent.com/pod-product-compliance
Lightning Source LLC
Chambersburg PA
CBHW080612220526
45466CB00010B/3327
9798396621459